G000080006

1 MONTH OF
FREE
READING

at

www.ForgottenBooks.com

By purchasing this book you are
eligible for one month membership to
ForgottenBooks.com, giving you
unlimited access to our entire
collection of over 1,000,000 titles via
our web site and mobile apps.

To claim your free month visit:

www.forgottenbooks.com/free789411

* Offer is valid for 45 days from date of purchase. Terms and conditions apply.

ISBN 978-0-483-57763-3
PIBN 10789411

This book is a reproduction of an important historical work. Forgotten Books uses
state-of-the-art technology to digitally reconstruct the work, preserving the original format
whilst repairing imperfections present in the aged copy. In rare cases, an imperfection in
the original, such as a blemish or missing page, may be replicated in our edition. We do,
however, repair the vast majority of imperfections successfully; any imperfections that
remain are intentionally left to preserve the state of such historical works.

Forgotten Books is a registered trademark of FB &c Ltd.
Copyright © 2018 FB &c Ltd.
FB &c Ltd, Dalton House, 60 Windsor Avenue, London, SW19 2RR.
Company number 08720141. Registered in England and Wales.

For support please visit www.forgottenbooks.com

· BY ·

REV. A. B. SIMPSON.

PUBLISHED BY
THE CHRISTIAN ALLIANCE PUB. CO.
692 EIGHTH AVENUE,
NEW YORK.

33961 X¹

¹ ⅋ 42

Copyrighted, 1892, by A. B. Simpson.

CONTENTS.

THE NAMES OF JESUS.

CHAPTER I.

THE WONDERFUL.

"His name shall be called the Wonderful Counselor, the Mighty God, the Everlasting Father, the Prince of Peace."

THE idea of a child king was not unfamiliar to the Old Testament. Little Samuel had been Israel's best prophet and judge; and young Josiah, wearing a crown at the tender age of five, was the best of Judah's kings after David.

In English history, the most honored name, perhaps, is Edward VI., the youthful king of the sixteenth century.

All these were types of Jesus, God's holy and anointed King. With beautiful simplicity, even after His resurrection and ascension,

the apostles speak of Him in their prayers to
the Father as "thy Holy Child, Jesus." He
Himself has told us that His best representative on earth is a little child : for, "He that
receiveth a little child in my name (that is,
belonging to me), receiveth me." And even
His Father in heaven is not ashamed to be
represented by the same little child. "He
that receiveth me, receiveth Him that sent
me."

There is nothing more beautiful in an old
and venerable man, than the simplicity of
childhood which often characterizes the
greatest minds. Perhaps when we meet with
our God, we will be most touched of all by
the simplicity of His presence. At least, it
is very beautiful to know that the Christ
who comes still to guide and govern us is a
child Christ, gentle as the touch of an infant's
hand, accessible as your own little ones, easy
to approach, simple and loving as an inno-
cent child; yet mighty as the Mighty God,
and the Everlasting Father. It is very
touching to notice in the last book of the

Bible (the Apocalypse), that Jesus is contin-
nally described by a diminutive term of
peculiar endearment; not the Lamb, as it is
translated in our version, but, literally, "the
little Lamb, the dear Lamb of God."

Let us look, however, at the other side of
the picture, and, as we do, let us carry with
us the conception of the child. Four illustrious and glorious names are here given to
Jesus.

1. "He is the WONDERFUL COUNSELOR."
This name has reference to His prophetic
work and office; for He is our prophet as
well as our king, the great teacher and guide
to His people. The term "counselor" has
reference to His guidance rather than to His
teaching. One may know much, and be able
to say much, and yet not be a good counselor.
Jesus is our wisdom, and leads His trusting
children in the right paths, wherein they
shall not stumble.

He is a Wonderful Counselor; first, He
often leads us contrary to the ideas, opinions,
and judgments even of wise men, and His

thoughts are as high above our thoughts as
the heavens above the earth. If He is our
guide He will often bid us do things which
prudence regards as folly, possibly as fanati-
cism ; but God will vindicate His own wisdom
in the end, and "Wisdom shall be justified
of her children." It seemed a very foolish
thing to the Canaanites for an army to march
seven days around their city walls, and then
simply blow their trumpets and shout; but
it was the wisest way to take Jericho. It
seemed a very foolish thing to ask a woman
—a widow—to give away her last handful
of meal to a stranger, when she and her boy
were starving; but it was the best way to
save her and her boy from starvation, and to
open the way for a continual supply for the
coming months. It seemed an absurd thing
for young David to face the giant Philistine
with a simple sling and stones; but it was
the only way by which he could have ob-
tained the victory. It seemed absurd to
commit to twelve fishermen the task of
evangelizing the world; but it was God's

wisdom, and it became God's mighty power. It may have appeared to Phillip very strange for the divine message to come to him to leave Samaria in the height of his great evangelistic work there, and go down into a lonely desert, where he could not expect to meet a soul; but it was God's way to preach the gospel to the Prince of Ethiopia, and, through him to the whole of Northern Africa. He leadeth us by a way that we know not; but it is ever the right way, and we shall thank Him at last that He has proved our Wonderful Counselor.

Again, He is a Wonderful Counselor because the people He leads are such weak and foolish people. When we commit ourselves to the guidance of Christ we become weaker in ourselves, even than others, ceasing to look to our own wisdom. Without His guidance we should indeed be utterly helpless, but this is our very strength. The little child who knows nothing of the way through the strange city is safer than the one who knows a little, because the latter is very apt to trust in its imperfect knowledge, and go astray; whereas, the former, knowing nothing, simply holds its mother's hand, and is safely led by one who knows better. And so it is said of the heavenly pathway, "The wayfaring man, though a fool, shall not err therein." "I am not sufficient," says Paul, "even to think anything as of myself; but my sufficiency is of God," and it is indeed wonderful how the most simple-hearted and uneducated minds are led by the Holy Spirit, not only into the full knowledge of God's Word, but kept from error and mistake, and guided safely through all the mazes of life's pathway!

Thirdly, This Counselor is wonderful in His patience and love. He is willing to take infinite trouble with us. Over and over again does He teach us the lessons we are so slow to learn. Over and over again does He repair our mistakes, and lift us up from our stumblings, and say to us, "How is it that ye do not understand?" There is no difficulty too intricate for Him to unravel. There is no little detail of life too petty for Him to take an interest in. There is no toil too tedious for Him to go through with us. There is no tangle too involved for Him to unthread and loose. There is no complication of difficult circumstances too extreme for Him to be willing to take hold of and lead us gently out into the light; and even our stupidity and rebellion have not always provoked Him to leave us; but He waits and loves us, and leads us, until at last He brings us into His perfect will and our hearts are ready to say, "Wonderful Counselor, patient Teacher, gentle Christ—who teacheth like Him?"

Fourthly, The best of all about this wonderful Counselor is that He does not merely tell us what to do, and give us a chart of the way, but He comes with us every step of the way and becomes our personal guide. Were you to go to Cairo and try to find from some Bedouin directions about the best way to cross the desert, or perhaps some map of the way or some itinerary of stations, he would laugh at you and say, "Why you will never find your way in that manner. I cannot tell you the way, but I will go with you and show you the way. I will be your personal guide." This is exactly what Jesus does. He says, "I am the way, and the truth, and the life." He says, when He putteth forth His own sheep, He goeth before them, and they know His voice, and a stranger will they not follow, for they know not the voice of strangers. "The Comforter, who is the Holy Ghost, shall abide with you forever, and He shall guide you into all truth."

How may we have the guidance of this wonderful Counselor ?

First, it is always indispensable that we shall be wholly yielded to follow His guidance and have a single purpose to please Him only. Willfulness will ever miss the way, but "the meek shall He guide in judgment, and the meek (the yielded ones, the little and bending hearts) shall He teach His way."

Secondly, we must bring to Him every particular need and acknowledge Him in all our ways, and He shall direct our steps. It will not do to take it as a matter of course, and say it will be all right anyhow, for the very thing in which we ignore Him is most likely to go wrong just because we have trusted in general and not specifically recognized Him.

Again, let us not expect startling revelations to come, but go by the simple light of His Word and our sanctified judgment and the voice of the Spirit as He speaks to us through quiet convictions, intuitions, and impulses. There are voices and voices. There is light which will come to us all, but it is false light. It may often be known by its blaze and glare. God's light is the soft and simple light which rests us, and brings the satisfying sense of His presence and peace.

Again, if we have His light, let us be willing to take it step by step. We shall not see all the way at once, but as we follow on we shall know the Lord in all His fullness, and all His purposes will ripen and unfold in all their fullness.

II. THE MIGHTY GOD.

He who is our Counselor is also abundantly able to carry out His plans, and He always follows up His directions with His strong and mighty hand. He never sends us on any path without standing by us and seeing us through. He who sends Israel around Jericho never fails to level the walls at the right moment. He who bids the people go forward into the sea, never fails to divide the floods. He who sends us through the waters and the fires, never fails to go before us and keep them from overflowing us. He who bids us march up against the gates of brass, never fails to precede us and break in pieces the brazen gates and make the crooked places straight. When the Holy Spirit is working in us, the mighty Providence of God is always working outside of us in perfect correspondence and preparation.

The Christ of the Gospels is the Jehovah of the Old Testament, the God who said to Jeremiah, Is there anything too hard for Him? He is the God of creation and of providence—the God who said to Moses, "I lift up my hand and say, 'I live forever,' and who is there that can deliver out of my hand?" He is able to control all the forces and elements of nature, able to restrain all the influences and movements of society, and turn the hearts of men at His pleasure, and overthrow their counsels and their works. He is able to save the lost, to pardon the guiltiest soul, to cleanse the blackest heart, to renew the most wrecked and ruined life. He is able to fill the heart of sorrow with untroubled gladness. He is able to take away the strongest tendencies to sin, and give the degraded and selfish soul the power to do that which is right and holy. He is able to satisfy our inmost, utmost being. He is able to put His own heart and nature in the most corrupt and helpless soul. He is able to touch the springs of physical life, and fill them with His own strength and healing. He is able to meet the temptations that overcome us, and to make us more than conquerors in all things through His love. He

is able to make even our little lives mighty
forces for everlasting good, and so clothe us
with His power that we shall be able to "open
the blind eyes, and turn men from darkness
into light, and from the very power of Satan
to God." He is still standing in our midst
and saying: "All power is given unto God
in heaven and in earth, and lo, I am with
you alway, even unto the end of the world."

He is greater than the greatest difficulty in
your life, the greatest sin, the greatest sorrow, the greatest failure. Over against the
things that are too strong for you, too hard
for you, from this day place Him, your
mighty God; only touch the hand of that
little Child, and lo, all the forces of Omnipotence, if need be, will be called forth to blast
the very rocks of adamant, to roll back the
tides of the ocean, to prepare the way for His
ransomed.

"When He makes bare His arm,
 Who shall His power withstand?
When He His people's cause defends,
 Who, who shall stay His hand?"

III. HE IS THE FATHER OF ETERNITY.

This is the true translation of this strange verse. It means that His being is unlimited; His years eternal; His element is a boundless one, and all His plans and thoughts are shaped and drawn on a gigantic, nay, an infinite scale. When we come into God, we come into the infinite. Eternity begins for us before time ends. The life we have now is eternal life. It takes hold upon illimitable things. There is about it a depth and a height, a length and a breadth that defy all calculations and computations, and the things that we take from God and do for God are eternal things. But a little we see now of what shall be revealed; but when He shall appear we shall be like Him. But let us build to-day for eternity. Let all our thoughts and plans and hopes be in view of the gigantic future, the colossal scale which is to unfold when we pass through the narrow gates of the earthly life into the illimitable beyond. Let us ever see ourselves as we shall be then, and our work as it shall seem then. Let us be content with nothing that is not going to last. Let us, too, belong to the ages to come, like Him. Ours is not an ephemeral breath of life, like the fluttering moth or butterfly, like the flashing meteor of the sky. We shall live when the sun is burned to ashes, and the stars have faded away, or taken on their new and everlasting forms; and could we see to-day, the scope of our future being, the height of our future glory, the grandeur of our future recompense, we would be afraid. We would be paralyzed with awe, and then with shame at the pettiness of our conceptions of God, and our expectations from Him; let us give our future to Him who is the Father of Eternity; let us lay up our treasures in hands that will give them back there, with the compound interest of their glory. Let us take more of the vastness rise to more of the boundlessness of thought and purpose, of love and faith, of joy and service, which He expects of those who would be worthy of His great and infinite heart that throbs within our breasts.

IV. HE IS THE PRINCE OF PEACE.

There is an allusion here to the kingdom of Solomon, whose name was significant of peace, and whose reign was typical of the coming King, his greater Son. It is to Him that the seventy-second Psalm is dedicated, with its beautiful words, "The mountains shall bring peace to the people, and the little hills, by righteousness. In his days shall the righteous flourish, and abundance of peace as long as the moon endureth."

His first conquest is through the gospel of peace. Having made peace through the blood of the cross, He came to preach peace to them that were afar off, and to them that were nigh. His coming was heralded with the words, "Peace on earth : good will to men." His last bequest before He died was, "Peace I leave with you, my peace I give unto you." His benediction as He arose and met them in the upper room was, "Peace be unto you." Being justified by faith, we have peace with God. He brings to the guilty heart the sense of pardon, and eternal

peace, and then He brings to the surrendered
heart the deeper rest that comes from passion and sin subdued and perfect trust in
Him as the sovereign and keeper of the soul.
He brings peace by conquest, but His conquest is that of love, the soul subdued into
harmony with Him with its own consent,
and every part of our being in harmony
with itself.

Nay, His glorious kingdom of peace ex-
tends further, for it brings us into perfect
harmony with all the relations of life and
circumstances that surround us, so that the
soul in which this glorious Prince reigns
easily adjusts itself to every situation, and
it finds God adjusting everything in its life
in glorious rest and fitness, so that it is true
that when a man's ways please the Lord He
maketh even his enemies to be at peace with
him; and where things are at war with us we
have a still higher victory, and can cry, with
the apostle, "We know that all things work
together for good to them that fear God, to
them that are the called of God according to

His purpose." "I have learned in whatsoever state I am therewith to be content. I know how to be abased, and I know how to abound ; everywhere, and in all things I am instructed to be full and to be hungry, both to abound and to suffer need. I can do all things through Christ that strengtheneth me."

And so the government shall be upon His shoulder ; and when it is, it is true that "of the increase of His government and peace there shall be no end." They that fully trust Him will find Him able to carry on His shoulder, not only the government of their own life, but of all the things that concern them ; and the more perfectly we submit everything to His control, the more sweetly shall we have cause to rest and sing,

> " I leave His sovereign will
> To choose and to command.
> With wonder filled, I ever find
> How wise, how strong His hand!"

Wonderful names! Wonderful Saviour, Counselor and Prince! Let us give Him the increase of the government and enter into

His perfect peace, and in a little while we shall find ourselves in the glorious millennial kingdom of His everlasting peace, where the last enemy shall be destroyed, and universal nature shall at length be brought into perfect and everlasting accord with His love and will, where war shall cease, and strife shall disappear, and sin shall come no more, and sorrow shall have passed away, and Satan shall be cast out, and storm and tempest shall never darken its sunny skies; but universal peace, and everlasting love, like a golden chain, shall bind the heavens and the earth together in one long endless kingdom of felicity and peace.

CHAPTER II.

THE ROCK OF AGES.

"Thou wilt keep him in perfect peace, whose mind is stayed on thee; because he trusteth in thee Trust ye in the Lord foreVer; for in the Lord JEHOVAH is eVerlasting strength." Isaiah xxvi: 3, 4.

THE literal translation of this beautiful verse, as it will be found in the margin of our English Bible is, "The Lord JEHOVAH is the Rock of Ages." This is the founda-ation of that beautiful hymn which is one that nine-tenths of the English-speaking Christians in the world would be sure to se-lect if asked for their six favorite hymns: a hymn without which any collection would be absolutely incomplete. The imagery is very familiar to every Bible reader. Rocks and mountains are associated with every important incident and epoch in the Bible. It was on Ararat that the new world began; on Moriah that the faith of Abraham was perfected; on Sinai that the law was given; on Horeb that the Tabernacle was designed; on Nebo that the Land of Promise was unveiled; on Zion that the capitol of Judah was fixed; on Moriah that the temple was reared; on Carmel that the nation of Israel was called to their covenant God; on Mount Hattin that Jesus preached His sermon; on Hermon that He was transfigured; on Calvary that He died, and from Olivet that He ascended. It is not strange, therefore, that the mountain and the rock have become favorite expressions of sacred things, for which their natural defences, their immutable and changeless features, their colossal strength, their lofty eminence, their wide reaching prospects of vision, and their beauty so specially fit them.

Hundreds of times the metaphor is repeated over and over again. "The Lord is our rock." "The rock of our heart." "The rock of our salvation." "The rock that is higher than we." "The shadow of a great rock in a weary land;" and here, sublimest

of them all, "The Rock of Ages." This is
the only passage in the Scriptures where
this particular phrase, so full of deep meaning and majesty, is found.

Like some sublime mountain face; like
yonder Profile mountain overhanging the
Franconia valley, and looking like a great
colossal face on the earth below, alone in its
grandeur; so this text is a mighty and isolated rock in which we can trace the face of
Jesus, our Rock of Ages; and, as we sit
down under its mighty shadow, as we rest
upon its velvet slopes, as we drink from the
crystal fountains that flow from its side, we
hear the sweet echo of our text: " Thou wilt
keep him in perfect peace, whose mind is
stayed on thee; because he trusteth in thee.
Trust ye in the Lord for-ever: for the Lord
JEHOVAH is the Rock of Ages."

I. THE ROCK.

Higher even than its fine natural sugges-
tiveness is the perfect scriptural significance
of this verse. It looks back to some of the

most instructive and striking types of the Old Testament.

1. It recalls the rock in Horeb, and speaks of Christ as our Saviour. "I would not have you ignorant," says the apostle, addressing us New-Testament Christians, "that our fathers did eat the same spiritual meat, and drink the same spiritual drink; for they drank of that rock that followed them, and that rock was Christ." Perishing with thirst, the Israelites were led by Moses to the face of the rock in Horeb. Then the law-giver lifted up his rod and smote the rock at God's command upon its naked face; and, lo! immediately it burst open, and from the cleft there poured a living stream, and through the camp it ran in rivulets and floods of living water, until the thirsty thousands drank and drank again, and gave their children and their cattle to drink until their thirst was fully satisfied; and they praised God for His great deliverance.

This incident has been applied with full

scriptural authority to the crucifixion of the Saviour. He, for us, was smitten by the rod of the Law-giver and Judge as our sacrifice and substitute, and from His pierced side there flows for us the water of life, where we can drink of His boundless mercies, His forgiving love, His renewing grace and thankfully sing,

> Rock in Horeb, riven for me
> By the law's avenging rod,
> Flowing from thy side I see
> Streams of water and of blood.
> And I wash my crimson soul
> Whiter than the wool and snow,
> While the cleansing waters roll.
> And the living fountains flow.

2. The Rock of Ages reminds us of the rock in Kadesh: the type of Christ, a fuller and more perfect Saviour. Forty years after the rock of Horeb was smitten, the camp of Israel came to Kadesh. The old story was repeated again. Thirsty and hungry they murmured instead of praying, and once again their law-giver led them to the rock. This time the command was different. He was not to smite the rock as before; but

simply to speak to it, and the promise was
given that the water should immediately
gush forth, In a moment of haste and disobedience he exceeded his orders, and smote
the rock repeatedly with words of irritation,
perhaps of unbelief.   God honored His
promise by sending the water abundantly
again; but He was grieved with His servant
for disobeying the explicit command; and
for this offence Moses was excluded from
the promised land. The waters, however,
came forth, and the people drank abun-
dautly, and the river continued to flow
through the desert.

This is the type of the deeper fullness of
Christ our Saviour, and of the infinite grace
of the Holy Spirit, which is simply waiting
the call of faith on the part of every believer.
This is not the atonement which first opened
the rock of salvation for us; but this is the
deeper fullness of the Holy Ghost, sanctify-
ing and satisfying the soul.

The word "Kadesh" means righteousness,
or holiness, and so this is the type of Christ

our Sanctifier and Satisfier. This does not teach us of the Holy Spirit procured and sent down from heaven through the finished work of Christ, but the Holy Spirit already given and simply waiting the call of faith to be received. We do not need now to smite the rock; to crucify Christ again, or to go through a desperate struggle and strain; but simply to look and live, to take and have, to speak the simple word of trust, "Come, Holy Spirit, Heavenly Dove," and lo! He answers quickly to our cry, and our prayer is changed to the song of praise:

> Rock of Kádesh, flowing still,
> From the Saviour glorified;
> All my empty being fill
> With thy Pentecostal tide.

3. The Rock of Ages looks back to another beautiful picture: "They drank of the rock that followed them." What can this mean? "Following rock." Not that the rock moved through the desert, but the river that ran from the rock followed them through the desert. The rock followed them with its floods of life and cleansing. The

Psalmist tells us the water ran in the desert like a river, and the historian tells us that when once in the desert they were perishing for want of water, they simply gathered in a little circle upon the burning sands, and with their staves dug a little well in the sand, and lifted up their voices to God in songs of praise; and lo! immediately the waters sprung up from the depths below, and overflowed again, as at Horeb and Kadesh, from the subterranean springs. So the Rock of Ages sends its living fountains all along our way, and although the desert may be all around us and the wells may all seem dry, yet faith has only to make room and lift up the song of praise even in the hottest desert, and lo! immediately the waters will spring forth in abundance, and we shall sing again:

> Following rock, from day to day, .
>   Sending forth on every hand
> Rivers all along the way,
>   Underneath the desert sand.
> Open deep the living well,
>   Where thy hidden fountains flow;
> Ever near thee let me dwell,
>   As I through the desert go.

4. But the Rock of Ages is also a sheltering rock. This is the rock of which the Psalmist cried, "Lead me to the rock that is higher than I." "He shall be as the shadow of a great rock in a weary land." A little rock only reflects upon us the more intensely the heat which it has absorbed; but the great rock drinks in the warm rays on one side, and on the other has a cooling shadow for the traveler who rests under its overshadowing cliffs. So, weak and selfish hearts only irritate us, and throw over us the reflection of their burdens; but Christ is the shadow of a great rock. Occupied every moment as He is with the cares of others, with the sorrows of a weeping world, with the myriad prayers that are every moment surging into His ears, with the dying cries and groans of sinking souls, with the despairing shrieks of the wretched ones that are every moment drifting into eternity, He is always at leisure for us. He is always at our call, and His whole heart is ever ready to comfort and rest us, as though there

were no others in the wide universe but we
requiring His sympathy and rest. Oh, the
delightful peace; oh, the safe refuge; oh, the
perfect security they enjoy who have found
their home within the cleft of the Rock of
Ages.

> Shadowing rock in weary lands,
>   Let me rest beneath thy shade;
> Traveling o'er the burning sands,
>   Shelter my defenceless head.
> Covert from the tempest rude,
> Refuge from the raging tide,
> Fortress when by foes pursued,
>   Let me in thy bosom hide.

5. But the Rock of Ages is also a foundation rock. It is a place to build upon. It is
the resting-place of faith and hope. There
trust finds its full assurance, as it leans upon
the promise, "He that believeth on the Son
hath everlasting life." There the soul can
struggle with self and sin as it reposes all
its weight upon the everlasting promise,
"The blood of Jesus Christ cleanseth us
from all sin." There hope anchors all her
cables, as she commits all her destinies, her
affections and her treasures to this immov-

able rock and cries, "I know whom I have believed, and I am persuaded that He is able to keep that which I have committed unto Him against that day." The mountains shall depart, and the hills shall be removed; but this rock shall stand. Our most substantial edifices shall crumble into dust; our oldest institutions shall vanish away; our securities and investments shall be ashes in the flames of a dissolving world; but the Rock of Ages will remain unshaken and immovable, and, standing upon it amid the awful roar of the last great convulsion, we shall indeed be able to say, "God is our refuge and our strength; a very present help in trouble; therefore will we not fear though the earth be removed and though the mountains be carried into the midst of the sea; though the mountains shake with the swellings thereof. God is in the midst of her; she shall not be moved; God shall help her, and that right early."

Rock of Ages, fixed and sure,
Be my faith's foundation stone;

Hopes we built on thee endure,
　　Stable as thy steadfast throne.
While my heart on thee is stayed,
　　Winds may howl and torrents pour;
I shall never be afraid,
　　I am safe forevermore.

Such are some of the scriptural suggestions of this beautiful name. There are further depths of significance in it that no words can fully unfold. It recalls to us not only the past associations of the Bible, but the past associations of the people of the church of God, and our own experience. It is the rock of the past. How touching it is to travel in Bible lands, and, as you sit down at the well of Nazareth or Bethlehem, to think of the thousands who in every generation have drunk of that fountain and rested at that well! There Abraham rested anddrank. There Jesus came as a little child with His mother. There crusaders, and pilgrims, and great travelers have quenched their thirst. How touching, how wonderful! It is the well of ages. This is the Rock of Ages.

How it quickens one's pulses and moistens one's eyes to go through the tower of London, and read upon the walls the last messages of saints and martyrs—the verses of Scripture which they were leaning their head upon in view of the scaffold or the stake upon the morrow! How wonderful to take that twenty-third Psalm and trace its record as it has been written, not only in Bibles and letters bathed in love and the prayers of human hearts and heavenly anointings; but as it has been written on prison walls and dungeon floors! Oh, how sacredly one feels as they read its verses, that they are treading on storied ground, and that every syllable is marked with the footprints of some sufferer or victor that has gone before!

And so, this Christ to whom we come has been the Christ of Ages. The comfort He gives us has been proved oft before. He is a tried stone; a sure foundation, and he that believeth on Him shall never be ashamed. He has been proved in temptation, in sickness, in sorrow, in death. Other generations

have proved Him. Our fathers and mothers
have proved Him. Our past trials have
proved Him.

> "Jesus, Jesus, how I trust Him,
>   How I've proved Him o'er and o'er,
> Jesus, Jesus, precious Jesus,
>   Oh, for grace to trust Him more."

And, as the Rock of Ages, He will live
through future ages. He covers all the future, and He is keeping all that can ever
concern us forevermore. Oh, let us trust in
the Lord JEHOVAH forever: for the Lord
JEHOVAH is the Rock of Ages.

II. THE REST.

"Thou wilt keep him in perfect peace
whose mind is stayed on thee, because he
trusteth in thee. Trust ye in the Lord forever."

This blessed rock is our place of rest. It
is a place of perfect rest. "Peace! Peace!!"
is the marginal and more beautiful translation of this picture of the Christian's rest.
There is a double peace. There is the peace
of conscience that comes with justification,

and the deeper rest of God that comes with His indwelling, and the best of this is that He keeps it. It is a peace that abides forever, and that keeps the heart in which it reigns: "For the peace of God, which passeth all understanding, shall garrison your hearts and minds through Christ Jesus."

But there are conditions on our part. The first is *trust*. This is the sweet Old Testement word for faith—its child phase. It is not so much the intellectual act of believing as the heart attitude of confiding and trusting.

The next condition is *staying*. We not only trust, but we stay trusting. There is a passive rest, which is the result of indolence and inaction. It is is simply drifting. The Christian's rest is an active reliance on the loving and everlasting arms of God. This will illustrate it. Look at yonder yacht running before the breeze. Let that helm go lax, and lo! the sails flap in the winds, and the boat drifts and tosses with the tide, dashed about at the mercy of the billows,

without any fixed course or steady poise.
This is the attitude of many a life—simply
drifting, trustless, restless, tempest-tossed,
and tending nowhere but to deeper unrest
forevermore. But look at that yacht now;
as the experienced seaman sits down at the
stern and puts his strong and steady hand
upon the helm, pressing hard against the
wind. See how the sails quickly fill and
lean against the wind, like white-winged
birds upon the air. Notice how the tossing
vessel rights up and sets her prow against
the waves in a steady course. Observe how
the driftings and tossings cease, and the
pitch and poise of the little ship are like the
movements of a thing of life. Notice how
swiftly she cuts her way through the raging
waters, obedient to the joint impulse of the
sail above and the helm astern. Notice how
the very winds that almost cross her path,
or blow in her very face, help her on her
course. Beautiful picture of the soul that
is stayed upon God! The pressure of His
providence, the very difficulties that confront

us but quicken our steadfast trust, and we
meet them with the firm hand and fixed
will of humble, holy confidence in God.
How the will springs into steadiness and
power! How its tossings are stilled, and its
whole movement is quieted, and intensely
alive and active, and yet intensely restful!
It presses on, like that noble little ship,
through wind and tide, in the will of God
and the work of life. This is the picture of
a soul stayed upon God.

There is, further, a distinct reference here
to the thoughts of the mind and their bearing upon the spirit of trust. It is the mind
that is stayed upon God. Just translate this
word " stayed " " stopped," and carry with
you the idea of a suspending of your busy
thoughts, and cares, and activities, and
you will understand better the prophet's
meaning. The rest of faith is usually hindered most by the restlessness of our ever
busy thought. We get to reasoning, ques-
tioning, wondering, fearing, looking forward
to this emergency and that contingency,

and our soul is disquieted by a whirlwind of
conflicting thoughts. God wants us to stop
thinking.

Not long ago a lady came to spend a week
or two in our Home, to learn the secret of
our deeper life in Christ. Her face was
clouded with care, and her heart was dis-
tracted with doubts, anxiety and fears.
She was really in danger of losing her mind
through spiritual unrest. She came to our
Friday meeting to be anointed for healing
of this terrible pressure upon her brain.
As we knelt by her side, we asked her if she
would promise the Lord to stop thinking
for a week. She said she could not; that
every instant she was like one swept by a
hurricane of troubled thoughts. We told
her she could and she must, that she needed
to set her will firmly in the strength of God,
and refuse to think; like the ill birds that
might beat their wings upon the window
pane, but she need not open the window
and let them in; like the wild billows that
might surge against the ship, and even flood

the deck, but she need not open the hatches and let them down into the cabin. She could simply stand guard at the door of her mind and refuse to receive these thoughts, to dwell upon them, to harbor them, to enter into sympathy with them. She could simply say, "I won't think," and as surely as she would do this, and hold steadily to this attitude, the habit would soon become established, and her thoughts would be controlled. But, she said, "shall I give up my good thoughts?" "Yes," our answer was, "everything at present, for all are unrestful. Even your good thoughts are evil, and when God gets you fixed in the habit of stillness, then He will breathe into you His thoughts without an effort upon your part." At length she reluctantly consented to make the promise and set her will like a flint, in the name of the Lord, against all thinking, and promised to learn to be perfectly still. Before the week had passed her whole face and heart were perfectly transfigured. "The peace of God that passeth all understanding," had taken possession of her soul, and she was rejoicing in the Lord and testifying to His victorious and keeping grace and power. Beloved, stay thy heart on God; not on thoughts nor feelings, but on that Presence that will possess you utterly, and fill you with that "peace that passeth all understanding," as you turn away from all else to Him alone.

Trust and rest in Christ forever,
    Lean thy head upon His breast;
Nothing from His love can sever
    Those who simply trust and rest.

Trust and rest in hours of sorrow;
    Every wrong shall be redressed,
In some happy, bright to-morrow,
    If you only trust and rest.

Trust and rest when all around thee
    Puts thy faith to sorest test;
Let no fear nor foe confound thee,
    Wait for God and trust and rest.

Trust and rest with heart abiding,
    Like a birdling in its nest,
Underneath His feathers hiding;
    Fold thy wings and trust and rest.

Trust and rest till gentle fingers
    Fold thy hands across thy breast,
While the echo softly lingers,
    Everlasting trust and rest.

CHAPTER III.

THE FIRST AND THE LAST.

"I am Alpha and Omega, the beginning and the end, the first and the last." Rev. xxii : 13.

AS WE think of the friends of life, how few there are that were linked with our earliest associations and memories! There was a period when every friendship began, and many of those we love the best we only knew for the first time a little while ago. But here a Friend addresses us who was before all other friends, who loved us long before we knew the love of brother, or even mother; long before even we were conscious of our own existence. "The Lord hath appeared of old unto me, saying, 'Yea, I have loved thee with an everlasting love.'" Jesus is indeed the First.

And then, how many of those that were the first in our life are not the last? The very mother on whose sweet face our eyes gazed before they recognized any earthly countenance, has long since passed from our view. But few of the friends of youth remain, and how many of the fondest attachments of life have been like rivers that run into the desert and are lost amid the sands; but here we have One who will be there at the close, who will remain when all others have passed away; for Jesus is the Last.

Oh! amid the passing years, and the passing forms of loved ones, and the changing scenes of life; how sweet it is to know that Jesus is the First and the Last! Let us gather up by the help of the Holy Ghost, some of the precious lessons of this wonderful name that covers all the present and the future.

I. THE FIRST.

1. This expresses the eternal pre-existence of Christ. We find Him constantly declaring this in His own addresses in the Gospel of John. "He was before me," is the wit-

ness of John to Him. "I came forth from the Father and am come into the world," is His own testimony. "Before Abraham was, I am." Even in the Old Testament we have some sublime pictures of the eternal Christ. "His name shall be the Everlasting Father (or the Father of Eternity), " is Isaiah's picture. "His goings forth have been of old, even from everlasting," is Micah's picture. "The Lord possessed me in the beginning of His way, before His works of old I was established from everlasting, from the beginning, or ever the earth was, when there were no depths, I was brought forth. When there were no fountains abounding with water, before the mountains were settled, before the hills, was I brought forth. When He prepared the heavens I was there. When He set a compass upon the face of the deep, then I was by Him as one brought up with Him, and I was daily His delight; rejoicing always before Him; rejoicing in the habitable parts of His earth, and my delights were with the sons of men." This is Solomon's

inspired picture of the eternal Logos, and
His ancient love to the world, and the men
that He was coming in the fullness of the
ages to redeem.

2. This expresses His pre-eminence. This
also is most clearly taught by the Holy Ghost
in the Scriptures, and claimed by Christ Himself. "That in all things He might have the
pre-eminence," is the Father's purpose re-
garding His dear Son, for His is the pre-eminence of deity. He is higher than all men,
higher than all angels; very God of very God;
the brightness of the Father's glory, the
express image of His person, the King of
kings and Lord of lords. There is no doubt
that this is what He claimed Himself, and
for this claim His life was threatened again
and again by the Jews, and taken at last in
His final judgment and crucifixion. "He
ought to die, because He has made Himself
the Son of God," was their charge. The
hands into which we commit our souls are
divine and infinite hands. The ransom which
has been paid for our sin is of the infinite

value of deity. The grace that is sufficient for our full salvation is the grace of the infinite God. The kinship to which He has raised us is nothing less than to be partakers of the divine nature, and sons and heirs of God, and joint heirs with Christ. Let us not fear to bring forth every diadem and crown Him Lord of all.

3. This expresses His relation to the work of creation and providence. This thought is expressed by the apostle Paul in his epistle to the Colossians in these strong and significant words: "For by Him were all things created that are in heaven, and that are in earth, visible and invisible, whether they be thrones or dominions, or principalities or powers; all things were created by Him and for Him; and He is above all things, and by Him all things consist." This expresses Christ's relation to the natural creation, and to the affairs of Providence. It was through His hand that the material universe was framed, and it is by His constant superintendence that the whole

machinery of Providence is carried on. By
Him all things consist, or, literally, "hang
together." He is the cohesive force that
holds the whole universe in order and harmony. All power is given to Him in heaven
and in earth. Like the Roman centurion,
all beings and forces are at the service of His
will, and He can say to this one, "Go," and
he goeth, or to this one, "Come," and he
cometh, and to all things, "Do this," and
they do it.

To Him we ascribe all the sublime de-
scriptions which Jehovah gives us in the Old
Testament of His sovereign power and glory.
Every robe of majesty and might will fit the
Son of God as perfectly as the Father, for it
is He that doeth according to His will in the
armies of heaven and among the inhabitants
of the earth, and none can stay His hand
from working, or say, "What doest thou?"
In the midst of the throne ever sits the en-
throned Lamb, while all angels and all creation sing in adoring reverence and love,
"Worthy is the Lamb that was slain to

receive power and riches and wisdom, and strength and honor, and glory and blessing. Blessing and honor and glory and power be unto Him that sitteth upon the throne, and unto the Lamb for ever and ever." This is our Christ: the first and the last.

4. This expresses also His relation to the Bible. Christ is first in these sacred pages. The one object of the Holy Scriptures is to reveal the person and portrait of Jesus. This is the key to its interpretation. This is the glory of its pages—Jesus in the story of creation, already planning the new creation; Jesus supreme above the ruins of the fall; Jesus in the ark, the rainbow and the dove; Jesus in the sacrifice on Mount Moriah, the ladder of Jacob, and the story of Joseph; Jesus in the Paschal lamb, the desert manna, the smitten rock, the pillar-cloud, the smoking sacrifice, the fragrant incense, the suffering scape-goat, the enrobed priest, the golden candlestick, the sacred ark, the sprinkled mercy seat, the hovering cherubim,

the awful Shekinah, the glorious tabernacle
and all its ministries and furniture; Jesus in
the land of promise, in the temple of Solomon, in the story of Joshua, the Psalms of
David, the throne of Solomon, the visions of
Isaiah, and the panorama of ancient prophecy as it unfolds toward the advent, the
manger, the cross and the throne; Jesus in
the Apostles; Jesus in the Apocalypse. The
testimony of Jesus is the Spirit of prophecy.
The face of Jesus can be traced like water
lines in fine paper back of every page, for
He is the Alpha and the Omega: the first
and the last of this Holy Book.

5. This expresses the relation of Jesus
Christ to redemption. He is the first in the
plan of salvation. Long ago He was heard
exclaiming, "Lo, I come; I delight to do thy
will, O God; mine ear hast thou bored." It
has all been accomplished through Him, and
His glory is all to return to Him, and He for
evermore to stand as the centre and head of
God's grandest work—the restoration of a
ruined race, the salvation of sinful men.

Christ is not only first in redemption: He is all. This wine press He hath trodden alone. None can share with Him this glory. His was all the cost. His alone the honor shall ever be. No name is so sublime in heaven as the Lamb. No song so loud as that which celebrates His redeeming love, and therefore all that receive this great redemption must give Jesus the supreme glory, or they cannot share it.

6. This expresses His relation to our individual salvation, for every soul must acknowledge Jesus as the first. "Ye have not chosen me, but I have chosen you," He tells us. The first desire to come to Him came from Him. The very hunger that longed for Him was His grace beginning to enter our hearts. He has loved us with an everlasting love, and, therefore, with loving-kindness has he drawn us. Not only has He pardon for us when we repent; but is exalted to give repentance to Israel and the remission of their sins. Not only will He fulfill our earnest prayers; but He maketh intercession within us with

groanings which cannot be uttered. Not only will He meet us in blessing if we will come to Him; but He will even take our will and work in us both to will and to do His good pleasure. His arms reach down to us at the lowest depth. His grace is beforehand in all its manifestations. Christ will take us at the very alphabet of Christian life, and from the very beginning will count us His disciples, and then will set us free. Oh, let us fully learn this precious truth, and always take Him for the very thing we need the most and the first, and even the very thing for which we ourselves are responsible, and yet insufficient; and He will not only do His glorious part, but He will enable us to do ours.

7. This expresses the relation of Christ to our Christian life and work. This is the true aim of a consecrated life—to make Jesus first. Let us give Him the first place in our heart, in our thoughts, in our aims and motives, in our plans, in our affections, friendships, occupations, our business, our

pleasures, our families, and our whole existence. Let us come to Him first for help
always. Let us bring to Him the very first
beginnings of temptation. Let us catch the
lions and the dragons while they are young,
and so shall we trample them under foot; and
we shall never see any old lions if we do so
without fail, for they will all be disposed of
before they have time to grow formidable.
Let us take to Him the very merest thing
that needs help, whether it be for soul or
body, for secular business or sacred experiences. Jesus first. Let this ever be our
simple watchword, and life's tangles will all
be unravelled, nay, will not have time to
grow serious, and so the touchstone which
will settle every question of perplexity and
duty will be Jesus first. Shall I do this?
Shall I please this person or Him? Shall it
be something else, or shall it be Jesus first?
Oh, how this will consecrate, elevate and
glorify our life, and enthrone Him and us
with Him, in a kingdom of constant peace
and victory! Beloved, shall we bring the

crowns and lay them at His feet, and write
on everything: "Henceforth, Jesus first."

II.   JESUS : THE LAST.

1. This implies the eternal existence of
Jesus. He is, as He himself expressed it,
alive for evermore; or, as the old prophet
put it still more sublimely, the Father of
eternity. It is glorious to have one that
covers all the future, and has in His hand
the scroll of every destiny and the control of
every future event. The Lamb in the midst
of the throne holds the sealed book of all our
destinies, and for evermore can fix every
event of our existence. No matter what is
coming, Jesus is coming with it. Though it
be trial, temptation, or death, He will be
there. The heavens and the earth shall pass
away; but He will remain. The friends we
have known will disappear ; but He will
abide. We will change; but He is the same
yesterday, to-day, and forever. The things
we commit to Him are committed against
that day. The interests that He is guarding

are safe forever. Beyond the smiling and the weeping ; beyond the parting and the meeting, He stands in eternity yonder, with our title and our crown safe in His keeping. How often have we felt that the present sorrow or even death were nothing if it were all safe beyond, if it would be all safe at last! Blessed be His name! He is the last, and His mighty works reach beyond all present vicissitudes, and guard our treasures and trusts for evermore. The things He gives us will stand. The things that are linked with Him are eternal.

> There is One amid all changes
> Who standeth ever fast ;
> One who covers all the future,
> The present and the past ;
> Jesus is the Rock of Ages,
> The first and the last.
>
> Jesus is the first ;
> Jesus is the last ;
> Trust to Him thy future,
> Give Him all thy past ;
> Jesus is the Rock of Ages,
> The first and the last.

2. Christ will finish His work in us, and carry to glorious consummation all that He

begins. Therefore, He is called the author and finisher of our faith. He who hath begun a good work within you will complete it unto the day of Christ. "The Lord will perfect that which concerneth me." "They who hear His voice," He says, "shall never perish, nor shall any one pluck them out of my hand." He takes us forever, and He will not leave us until He has done all that He has spoken to us of. He never leads His flock out to desert them in the hour of need. He never leads us out into the difficult enterprise, without promising to stand by us and crown our work with success. He says of every true enterprise begun in His name and at His bidding, "The hands of Zerubbabel have laid the foundations of this house, his hands also shall finish it, and they shall know that the Lord of Hosts hath sent me unto you."

3. Christ is not only the finisher of our life and work; but Christ himself is the end and substance of all things, and when we are done with things and people and see Him

as He is, we shall find that His heart was the fountain of all love, His smile the substance of all joy, His life the life of all life, Himself the first and the last of everything, and we shall have nothing that is not part of Him and linked with Him. Every face we see shall simply reflect His beauty. Every joy we shall feel shall be but a radiation from His heart. Every glory we shall wear shall be but a reflection of His holiness. Every throb of our immortal life shall be but a pulsation of His being, and Christ shall be all, and in all, and we shall have reached the last line of the old chorus, "Everything in Jesus, and Jesus in everything." So let us step out into another year, writing over every day and hour and moment, "Jesus first," and we shall find surely that Jesus is the last.

CHAPTER IV.

CHRIST THE LIVING WAY.

"Having, therefore, brethren, boldness to enter into the holiest by the blood of Jesus, by a new and living way, which He hath consecrated for us, through the veil, that is to say, His flesh; and having an high priest over the house of God; let us draw near with a true heart, in full assurance of faith, having our hearts sprinkled from an evil conscience, and our bodies washed with pure water. Let us hold fast the profession of our faith without wavering (for He is faithful that promised); and let us consider one another to provoke unto love and good works." Heb. x: 16–24.

THESE profound words tell us of five things: two things which we have, and three things which we are to do.

I. THE THINGS WE HAVE.

1. We have boldness to enter into the holiest by the blood of Jesus. We see before us a model of the ancient Tabernacle —God's most perfect type of Christ and our Christian life. Entering the gate and

the court, we are beside the altar of sacrifice and the laver of cleansing, which tell us of Christ's atonement for our sins, and the Holy Spirit's cleansing work in our hearts. Passing still further in we come to the Holy Place, through the door; and the candlestick, the table of shew bread, and the altar of incense proclaim to us in symbol, the illumination of the Holy Spirit in the heart where He dwells, the living bread with which Jesus nourishes those who abide in Him, the sweet communion with God which that altar and its incense set forth, and all that is meant by abiding in the secret place of the Most High, and dwelling in intimate fellowship with Jesus.

Still further in stands the Holy of Holies, separated only by the veil, and entered only by the High Priest once a year on the Great Day of Atonement. It is the symbol of the presence and glory of God, of the heavenly world and of the access into it, which even here we may enjoy in the sweet fellowship of Jesus. All this imagery is

called up by the text. Dean Alford trans-
lates the phrase, "Holy Places," and so
makes it mean all the chambers of the
Tabernacle, even the court, and including
the Holy of Holies. Thus it would express
all the fullness of our spiritual privileges in
Christ—the life in heavenly places in Christ
Jesus, as the apostle calls it in the Epistle to
the Ephesians. Specially, however, it refers
to the inner chamber, and expresses our
complete and unobstructed access to all the
fullness of God.

Had you stood in that Tabernacle three
thousand years ago, you would have seen
the view of that inner chamber obscured by
the heavy veil covered with its symbolical
embroideries which hung between: this veil
and its embroideries speaking of Judaism
and its types, which as yet obstructed the
full view of the heavenly world, and yet in
a measure foreshadowed them. Had you
stood in that Tabernacle, however, on the
Great Day of Atonement, you would have
seen a solitary man, robed in priestly gar-

ments, pass through that veil with a censer full of burning coals and a bunch of hyssop saturated with sacrificial blood, and for a moment stand within that holiest place and sprinkle that altar with the blood while he made intercession for the waiting congregation outside; and then you would have seen him retire with solemn awe and close the veil behind him, and enter no more until the year was ended.

All this received its literal fulfillment on that day when, outside the eastern gate of Jerusalem, the Son of God died on Calvary, and His mortal flesh was rent by the death-stroke. Suddenly the watchers in the temple beheld that mighty veil, that hung so high that human hands could not have reached it, rent asunder from top to bottom, proclaiming that from henceforth the way to the holiest of all was opened, and that there was no barrier between the believing sinner and the holy God. This is indeed true.

The way is opened to us to the altar of

atonement for full and complete forgiveness, to the laver of cleansing for the washing of regeneration, and the renewing of the Holy Ghost, to the golden candlestick for the fullness of the Holy Spirit's light and teaching, to the table of shew bread for the living bread which will sustain us in our spiritual and physical being, to the altar of incense for Christ's own intercession for us, and constant access ourselves for communion with God.

Nay, more, the ark of the covenant, guarding and keeping for us God's holy law tells us of our access to complete sanctification in Christ, and the blood of sprinkling that keeps us ever accepted in His sight, nay, even we may come to the very Shekinah of His presence to walk ever in the light of His countenance and dwell in the bosom of His love. Not timidly and with a sense of unworthiness are we to walk, but boldly, knowing that we are unworthy, but that Jesus Christ has purchased for us all these redemption rights, and that we may fully claim them without doubt nor fear. We have boldness by the blood of Jesus. We can take as much as that is worth. We were unworthy, but all has been covered by His satisfaction. We could not have come ourselves, but He has become our living way. We could not have put that veil aside, but God rent it from top to bottom through the death of His dear Son, and our crucifixion with Him, "for the veil is His flesh."

In His earthly body He represented our sinful humanity, and was bearing in His own person all the liabilities of lost men, and was really counted a sinner in the eye of the law of God. That flesh stood between us and God, therefore it had to die in place of the guilty race, and when Christ's flesh was crucified on Calvary, it was the same as if the guilty race had been judged and slain. The obstruction was immediately removed, and the way for access into the presence of God was opened.

There is a very deep spiritual application in all this for us. Before the holy of holies can be fully opened to our hearts, and we can enter into the immediate presence and communion of God, the veil upon our hearts must rend asunder, and this comes as it came on Calvary—by the death of our flesh. It is when we yield our own natural self to God to die, and He slays us by the power of His Spirit, that the obstruction to our communion with God is removed and we enter into its deeper fullness. The greatest hindrance to our peace and victory is the flesh. Whenever the consciousness of self rises vividly before you, and you become absorbed in your own troubles, cares, rights or wrongs, you at once lose communion with God, and a cloud of darkness falls over your spirit.

There is really nothing else that hurts or hinders us but this heavy weight of evil, this seed of Satan, this embodiment of the inmost essence of sin, this great mimic and antagonism of God, whose place it usurps, whose throne it claims, whose perogatives it dares to monopolize. We can never rend it asunder, but the Holy Spirit can. It dies only on the cross of Jesus and on the pierced bosom of His love, under the fire of His descending Spirit. Bring it to Him, give Him the right to slay it, reckon it dead, and then the veil will rend asunder, the Holy of Holies will open wide, the light of the Shekinah will shine through all the house of God, and the glory of heaven shall be revealed in your heart and life, and your inmost being become like that ancient Tabernacle when illuminated by the golden candlestick and the Shekinah of God's visible presence.

2. We have a High Priest over the house of God. Not only have we a home to shelter us, but we have an Elder Brother to welcome and love us.

The ministry of the ancient high priest was very important. It was he that opened the way into the holiest, and made reconciliation for the sins of the people. So our great High Priest has opened for us the way, and keeps it ever open, "and ever liveth to make intercession for us." It is His business to settle for us the question of our sins, and keep us cleansed from their power, and saved from their effects. The time to go to Him is not when you feel strong in your victories, but when baffled, defeated, and crushed by temptation and conscious unworthiness. He that washed the disciples' feet still stands in the heavenly court girded with the towel of priestly service, and with open bosom ready to pour His precious blood over all your stains. Let us, therefore, come boldly to the throne of grace, even to obtain mercy, as well as to find grace to help in time of need.

The ancient priest also ministered to the suffering and the sick. It was his business to inspect the leper, to offer the sacrifices for his cleansing, to pronounce him clean; and so our great High Priest is also our great Physician, and heals all our diseases, comforts all our sorrows, and binds up our broken hearts. He is able to be touched with the feelings of our infirmities, for He was in all points tempted like as we are, yet without sin.

Also, He bore upon His shoulders, and upon His breast in jewelled letters, the names of Israel's tribes, and so Christ bears us upon the shoulders of His strength and the bosom of His love in unceasing faithfulness and unfailing strength. He presents our prayers before the throne with acceptance to His Father and ours. He keeps our relations with God always right. He remembers us in constant intercession, even when we ourselves may not know our need, nor what to pray for as we ought.

In a word, He superintends, and carries on the entire business of our spiritual life, and is for us the author and finisher of our faith. We have such a High Priest. He is there in our behalf. He has been appointed by His Father for this great trust. He has given Himself to us for this great business. We have accepted Him as such. He belongs to us. Let us make use of this glorious opportunity, and "seeing we have an High Priest, who has passed into the heavens, Jesus the Son of God, let us hold fast our profession, and let us come boldly up to the throne of grace, that we may obtain mercy, and find grace to help in time of need."

II. WHAT WE SHOULD DO.

1. Let us draw near. This is to say, let us not live a distant, cold, and timid life, but let us enter into all the fullness of our privileges, and live in the intimate friendship of our Saviour. Let us come with a single purpose to please and obey Him with a true heart, and an honest single aim. Let us come in full assurance of faith, not timidly dreading a reproof nor a blow but, sweetly knowing that we are welcome, and like a happy child pressing right up into the bosom of our Father. And even if we are conscious of unworthiness, let us come with a heart sprinkled from an evil conscience, and bodies washed with pure water. There is cleansing for us, if we have erred, in that precious blood, and that renewing Spirit's grace, and not even our

imperfections should keep us back from communion with God and the joy of His presence.

It is a very beautiful provision of the olden time that the blemished priest might not minister at the altar, but he may eat of the priestly bread. A broken limb or a crooked joint disqualified him from standing at the altar as an officiating priest, but not from entering the Holy place, and feeding upon the provisions for the priesthood. Beautiful token that .Christ's most imperfect children are welcome to His love, and grace, and may ever draw near for His help and comfort, and while this must not encourage weakness, yet let it ever keep from discouragements, and constrain us to draw still nearer to His breast, and so to live that we shall ever please Him, and not have sin to bring Him, but grateful love and holy service.

2. "Let us hold fast the profession of our faith, without wavering, for He is faithful that promised;" or rather, let us

hold fast the faith, or hope which we have professed. This hope of ours and this faith refer to the great eternal goal of faith and hope—our complete salvation through Christ Jesus. But it also applies to every confidence which God has given to us, and every promise which He has permitted us to claim. Let us stand steadfastly in the trust which He has given us, and let us do so without a faltering movement nor a trembling fibre. Let us stand unshaken in our confidence, and let us do so because He stands firmly at the other end. The cable yonder is fastened round the throne. Let it be fastened around our hearts in inflexible and immovable security, and thus standing upon His promises and holding fast our confidence, He is not hindered on His side in fulfilling all His purposes of blessing.

3. "Let us consider one another to provoke unto love and to good works." Such glorious privileges should make us unselfish and devoted, and find expression in lives

of loving service. As travelers ascending dangerous mountains tie their bodies together with strong cords, so that if one should fall the others will support him; so God has linked our hearts and lives together by innumerable cords of sympathy, suffering and mutual influence; and if one member suffers all suffer. Particularly are we, who have entered into the holiest and are walking into the inner presence of God, expected to be loving, and cheerful, and helpful to one another, and to bear the burdens of the weak and suffering, The best evidence you can give that you are a strong Christian is to bear the infirmities of the weak, and not to please yourself, "even as Christ pleased not Himself; but, as it is written, the reproaches of them that reproach thee fall on me." Therefore let us consider one another, hold up each other, bear one another's burdens, and so fulfill the law of Christ. Let us carry one another in the sweet ministry of prayer. Let us be patient with each other. Let us be very considerate of each other's faults and failings, and let us prove that we have indeed a deeper life and a fuller blessing, by pouring it out abundantly on those who lack.

Such, then, beloved, are our privileges and responsibilities. Let us more fully possess the former, and more faithfully shall we perform the latter. More intimately let us draw near, more constantly let us dwell in the secret of His presence, and more faithfully shall we fulfill our duties to others in every earthly relationship, and let us do this so much the more as you see the day approaching. Our Lord is coming ere long, and this blessed hope, if fully realized, will make all our trials, irritations and provocations seem light and small in comparison with the one great object of winning His approval and wearing the crown which He will give to Him that overcomes.

CHAPTER V.

CHRIST OUR SURETY.

"He is the surety of a better covenant, which was established upon better promises."

"For all the promises of God in Him are yea, and in Him Amen, unto the glory of God by us."

"He hath made with me an everlasting covenant, ordered in all things, and sure."

COVENANTS are more common in Oriental countries, and more sacred than in our modern life. The Arab chief will guard with his life the person with whom he has made the covenant of bread and salt. God has accommodated Himself to human speech and customs by revealing the glorious plan of mercy to us under the figure of a covenant, and has bound Himself to us by bonds so secure and sacred that they are an anchor of the soul, both sure and steadfast, if we have fled for refuge to the hope set before us in the gospel.

I. THE COVENANT OF REDEMPTION.

This takes us away back to the ages before the fall, and the revelation of God's mercy. In the counsels of eternity the covenant was made between the Father and the Son. Then it was that foreseeing the ruin that was to come upon the human race through the awful power of sin, God the Father entered into a covenant with His beloved Son, guaranteeing to Him, on condition that He should assume the liabilities and the nature of the fallen race, to give to Him for them a complete salvation. On the part of Christ it was necessary that He should take the sinner's place, that He should stoop from His high and exalted position and become, not only a man, but a despised and rejected man, a man of sorrows, should die upon the cross as a sacrifice for sin, should bear the taunts and cruelties of man, the pains of death, the assaults and insults of the devil and all his legions, should go down into the gloomy regions of the dead; and then should come forth, and for ages sit upon the throne of intercession as a merciful High Priest, bearing the burdens of His people, making continual intercession for them, enduring their provocations, infirmities and failures, and guarding them with unceasing love, until His work might be completed in all their lives. On the Father's part, He promised on account of the fulfillment of these conditions, He should give eternal life to all that received His Son, and freely forgive and justify them from all their transgressions, and create within them a new heart, and give them His Holy Spirit, should sanctify them and perfect them in holiness, should supply to them all needed grace, power, love, and blessing, should accept them as the sons of God, and make them the heirs of His glory, and partakers of the divine nature, and at last raise them from the dead, and glorify them with Jesus in the ages to come, with a place of honor and blessing higher than Adam ever knew, higher than angels shall ever possess, and more than compensating for all the evils and miseries of the fall. This covenant Jesus Christ accepted. "Lo, I come!" was His glad answer, "I delight to do thy will, oh, my God: yea, thy law is in my heart." And so He came, and lived and loved, and died, and at last could say, in His closing prayer, as He committed His work to the Father, "I have finished the work that thou gavest me to do; and on the cross could shout, "It is finished."

Then the Father put His seal upon the finished work by raising Him from the dead, and so declaring forever that the covenant had been fulfilled, the conditions met, and the great redemption completed. Christ's ascension from the tomb was the seal of this; the coming of the Holy Ghost on the day of Pentecost was a second seal; the conversion of every believer since has been a further seal that the covenant is ratified, and forever holds fast. Every answer to prayer in the name of Jesus, every blessing that comes to our spiritual life, is an echo from the cross repeating, "It is finished;"

and we know that the covenant is fulfilled, and, "in all things ordered and sure." This is the ground of our salvation. It is not because we have a covenant with God, but Jesus has; and we simply accept Him, and we come into His covenant, for He could say to the Father, "Thou hast given Him power over all flesh that He should give eternal life to as many as thou hast given Him;" and then He could add, "Keep through thine own name those whom thou hast given me, that they may be as one, even as we are."

Our salvation, therefore, is wholly dependent upon our accepting Jesus, and this brings to us all the promises of the covenant that He has ratified and fulfilled. Therefore, "All the promises of God in Him are yea, and in Him Amen." Therefore, to the last moment of our life, we have no personal claim upon God for anything. Everything we receive is the infinite mercy of God in Christ and for His sake; and to the last breath of life, we shall never receive anything that is not the pure undeserved mercy of God for His sake. How very simple this makes salvation! How very strong our consummation in Christ? How very sacred our hope! How mighty the anchor that holds us in the storm of temptation, and doubt, and fear!

II.   THE REVELATION OF GOD'S COVENANT.

The law of Moses was not the covenant of God which He designed to be His permanent bond of union with His people. It was simply a temporary revelation, similar to the covenant of works made at the creation of man, which God knew they would not keep, and which was designed, not to save men, nor to sanctify them, but to reveal to them their sin, and show them the need of a higher covenant of grace and mercy in Christ, even the covenant of grace which Christ has brought in.

The first full revelation of God's covenant of grace was made to Abraham; and the covenant of Abraham still holds good for all believers. This was not intended for the

Jewish people exclusively, but it was designed to include all the children of faith, of whom Abraham was the spiritual father. This the apostle clearly teaches us in the epistle to the Galatians, where he tells us that "they which be of faith, the same are the children of Abraham. And the scripture, foreseeing that God would justify the heathen through faith, preached the gospel unto Abraham, saying, In thee all nations shall be blessed. So, then, they which be of faith are blessed with faithful Abraham."

The essence of the covenant with Abraham was the promise of the seed, and this was Christ, so that Abraham's covenant was just that Jesus was to come and do all things in accordance with the eternal covenant of redemption, of which we have previously spoken. This covenant, Abraham received in the simplest way by naked faith, but he did not do anything to deserve it. He just believed God. God came to him with a revelation of His promise and mercy, and Abraham accepted it like a child and began

to act accordingly, and his life was simply
one of trust and trustful obedience, and for
this, God blessed him with His friendship and
made him father of all who have since been
received into that covenant friendship.

Much more fully in the later scriptures do
we find this covenant unfolding. Particularly in the writings of Jeremiah does God
reveal to His people, in the darkest hour of
their sin and suffering, His future plans of
grace and mercy. "Behold the days come,"
we read in Jer. xxxi: 31, "that I will make
a new covenant with the house of Israel, and
with the house of Judah; not according to
the covenant that I made with their fathers,
in the day that I took them by the hand
to bring them out of the land of Egypt;
which my covenant they brake, although I
was an husband to them, saith the Lord.
But this shall be the covenant that I shall
make with the house of Israel; After those
days, saith the Lord, I will put my law in
their inward parts, and will write it in their
hearts; and will be their God, and they

shall be my people. And they shall teach no more every man his neighbor, and every man his brother, saying, Know the Lord: for they shall all know me, from the least of them to the greatest of them, saith the Lord; for I will forgive their iniquity, and I will remember their sin no more."

That this is the covenant of the gospel is perfectly certain from the fact that in the epistle to the Hebrews it is twice quoted by the Holy Ghost as the rule of God's dealings with His people to-day, and as the bond into which He brings them in Jesus Christ, who is the surety of this better covenant established upon better promises.

The promises of this covenant are very wonderful. The first of them is our sanctification. It is very glorious that the thing that God first undertakes to do is to make and keep us right. Instead of giving us an outward law and compelling us to keep it without power, He promises to put it in our hearts, to make us live it, to make us incorporate it into our being, to enshrine it in our affections, to make it our very nature, until we shall live it and keep it, spontaneously, joyfully, lovingly, and with our whole heart. This is what the Holy Spirit does and therefore, on the day of Pentecost, He came on the anniversary of the giving of the law to be the inner law of holiness and power in every believer's heart.

Next, He promises to be our God. He next comes to us to be our all-sufficiency for every need. He lets us own Him and possess Him as our God, and use Him in His infinite resources for every need. Further, He promises that we shall know the Lord for ourselves, and have His light and guidance, not being dependent upon others to teach, but receiving directly from His will and mind for us. And finally, it includes complete forgiveness and eternal obliteration of all sin and transgression, the blotting out of the past, our entire justification, and the treating of His children as if they had not sinned. Beloved, will you take this mighty covenant? It is yours by purchase of the Redeemer's blood; and if you simply accept Jesus, "How shall He not with Him also freely give us all things?" and what can you need besides this mighty provision?

III. THE SECURITY OF THIS COVENANT.

He says, "It is an everlasting covenant, in all things ordered and sure." Again He says, "The mountains shall depart, and the hills be removed; but my kindness shall not depart from thee, neither shall the covenant of my peace be removed, saith the Lord that hath mercy on thee."

The reason it is so secure is because it is not dependent upon us at all, but on its great surety, the Lord Jesus Christ. If we were dependent upon our works in the slightest particular, we should fail and wreck all our prospects; but He has confirmed it and therefore it must stand, and if we simply stand in Him, trusting and following Him, He will accomplish all its provisions in us and for us. Therefore the apostle says, "Therefore it is of faith that it might be of grace, to the end that the promise may be sure to all the seed." If it had been of works it could not have been sure; but it is by faith, and faith is nothing but receiving a gift and thanking Him for it, and continuing to trust Him for it.

Again, it is sure because God not only promised it, but He has covenanted it and sworn to it. The very strongest language has been employed to emphasize the absolute security of this great promise of mercy, "That by two immutable things, in which it was impossible for God to lie, we might have a strong consolation, who have fled for refuge to lay hold upon the hope set before us in the gospel." If we simply have fled for refuge, and are holding fast to our hope in Christ and to Christ our hope, the anchor must hold amid all the storms of doubt and temptation.

Again, it is secure because it is based on God's pure mercy, and not upon our deserving. He takes us from the beginning and He holds us to the end as the children of His mercy. It is not merely that He takes us at first in mercy and afterwards treats us according to our deserving, but all the way along we must recognize ourselves as worthless and undeserving, living upon His mercy, and saved and sanctified through His free grace. Therefore our very sanctification, instead of being a merit, is simply a richer mercy, and the apostle says, "That they which have received abundance of grace and the gift of righteousness shall reign in life by one Jesus Christ."

Oh, it is so sweet to feel that we are ever lying in the bosom of His mercy, and that we claim His great salvation with the consciousness of our nothingness and worthlessness, and yet of our infinite and everlasting life in Christ! Therefore the apostle has said that "all the promises of Him are yea, and in Him Amen. Everything we ever claim in answer to believing prayer must come through His mercy and covenant; but we claim them all for this great reason, "for Jesus' sake." And they all are yea at the beginning, and shall be Amen at the end; for we simply claim them and hold to them for His sake and in His name. He is the surety of our covenant.

Or, shall we say that the yea is God's assurance, His repeated word, His second immutable thing, and the Amen is the echo of our faith as it takes Him at His word, and declares it shall be done? Thank God for His secure and everlasting covenant. Thank God that in Christ it covers us. Beloved, let us take it, and let our names be written to it afresh, and cover with it all our future way. Let us cover with it our sins behind, our hearts within, our way before, our hours of temptation and conflict, our hours of suffering and trial, our hours of prayer, our hours of service, our ignorance and helplessness, our perils, and our paths of difficulty all the way down to the tomb, all the way up to His coming. It covers all right up to the throne; and the anchor will hold, until, within the vail all the storms are past, and the surges swell no more, and we shall say around the throne, with a great shout, "Salvation unto our God who sitteth upon the throne, and unto the Lamb."

"Beloved, have you been thinking mostly of your faith and your works, and your fidelity to God? Have you not, perhaps, been somewhat under the covenant of Sinai, and therefore weakened and crushed? Oh! hasten to Calvary, and take refuge in the hope set before you in the gospel, with a heart humbly and simply yielded to Jesus. Take His great covenant rather than yours, and rest in His faithful and everlasting pledge to carry you through all, and say, "Who shall separate us from the love of Christ." It is not the babe's arms that hold the mother; but the mother's arms that hold the babe.

"It's not my love to thee,
  That I delight to tell,
But on thy love, O Christ to me,
  How I delight to dwell!

Ere the creation rose,
  Or angels sang above,
The records of the past disclose,
  Thine everlasting love.

Lord, help me to believe
Thy wondrous love to me,
So shall my heart more fully give,
Thine own love back to thee."

CHAPTER VI.

CHRIST OUR PASSOVER.

" Purge out, therefore, the old leaven, that ye may be a new lump, as ye are unleavened. For even Christ, our passover, is sacrificed for us : therefore let us keep the feast, not with old leaven, neither with the leaven of malice and wickedness; but with the unleavened bread of sincerity and truth." 1 Cor. V: 7, 8.

THE Jewish Passover is one of the most lasting memorials of God's covenant with His ancient people. After three thousand years have passed away, after temple and tabernacle worship have ceased, after the scattering of Israel's sons in another land, after the cessation of sacrifices and ceremonial worship in almost every other particular, after the treading down of Jerusalem for nearly twelve centuries, you can still find as every Nisan returns, every Hebrew household in the world gathering around their table at the evening hour of the passover week, eating the flesh of the lamb and the

unleavened cakes with bitter herbs, while
the father of the household, with lighted
candle, passes through the chambers and
searches under every article of furniture to
see if he can find a single particle of leaven,
and then solemnly pronounces that all the
leaven is cast out. They sit down together
under the sprinkled blood, and partake of
the paschal supper. How vividly it all interprets the words of our text, "Christ our
Passover is sacrificed for us; therefore let us
keep the feast, not with old leaven, neither
with the leaven of malice and wickedness,
but with the unleavened bread of sincerity
and truth!"

I. THE PASCHAL LAMB.

In the book of Exodus we find the story
of the first passover. It was the beginning
of months to Israel, even as the acceptance
of Christ as our Saviour is to us the beginning of life's record in its eternal form.

1. The first thing was the selecting of the
lamb. It was chosen on the tenth day of

the month, the time suggesting the fullness of the time when God sent forth His Son. The lamb was first separated and set apart for three days and a half under the observation of all the people, and known to be without blemish and without spot. Even so at His baptism on the banks of the Jordan the Lord Jesus Christ was set apart by the Holy Ghost for three years and a half to the observation of all men, before He was sacrificed for the sins of the world.

2. Again, the lamb was unblemished. So Christ was perfectly harmless, and undefiled, and separate from sinners, with no guilt of His own to expiate, and therefore wholly free to be an atonement for the world. His perfection was witnessed by all men. His blamelessness could be seen in all possible circumstances. His life was open as the noontide blaze, and none could find fault with Him in aught that He ever said or did. Even in the judgment of His enemies, it was the most perfect and beautiful life ever lived below the skies. Even if

there was no historical Christ, the Christ of the gospels is a faultless and irreproachable picture, which infidelity gazes upon with astonishment and admiration.

3. The lamb was next slain by the congregation of Israel. And so Christ was sacrificed by the decision of the Jewish Sanhedrim and the act of the entire nation; and was thus in some sense the public and official oblation made by them for their sins. The words of Caiaphas just before his death had a peculiar significance, which he did not understand. "It is expedient," he said, "that one shall die for the people, and that the whole nation perish not." And so Judaism, like the great High Priest, offered up its own Messiah as a sacrifice and an offering for the sins of the world; and as they gazed upon the quivering bosom, and the failing breath, and the flowing blood of that gentle lamb, how vividly they must have realized the meaning of sin and the cost of salvation! Even so we still behold the dying agonies of the

Lamb of God, and in the memorial of His
death, in some measure realize afresh "He
was led as a lamb to the slaughter, and as a
sheep before his shearers was dumb, so
opened He not His mouth," until we see,

> "Mercy's streams in streams of blood,
> Plenteous grace our soul bedewing,
> Plead and claim our peace with God."

What was the full significance of that
death? It was the substitute for their death.
The first-born of Egypt fell before the de-
stroyer's stroke; but that death took the
place of their own death, and they escaped.
And so, for our life His life is the sacrifice,
and with that blood over us our spiritual life
is redeemed. and our physical life is safe until His will shall call it home. No destroying
angel can touch us, though he may hover
near, so long as we are under the blood, and
that death is our substitute and sacrifice.

4. The sprinkling of the blood. The death
of the lamb was followed by the sprinkling
of the blood upon the door posts and lintel of
every home. It is not enough that Christ

should be sacrificed: He must also be appropriated by each for himself and herself. It is very sweet to know that the sprinkling was not done by other hands, but each household sprinkled its own doors; and so can each of us apply to ourselves the precious blood of our Redeemer. It is freely shed for all, and each of us can take it as freely as we may. How precious to know that this blood is for us still! Take it, dear sinner, and you can cover yourself from this very moment, so that no angel of destruction can touch your being; but you shall stand sheltered by the very throne of God from all harm in the precious blood of Christ. "We are come to the blood of sprinkling which speaketh better things than that of bulls." Have you applied it? Apply it now, and ever walk under its sheltering, cleansing covering.

II. THE FEAST.

Not only was there a sacrifice, but there was also a feast. Not only was the blood shed for the remission of our sins, but the life of our dear Lord is also given us for our life. They were to eat the flesh of the lamb as well as sprinkle its blood. We need not say that this represents Christ's own very life given to us as the food and nourishment of our whole being. "I am the living bread, he that eateth me shall live by me." "The bread that I shall gi. e is my flesh, that I shall give for the life of the world, for my flesh is meat indeed, and my blood is drink indeed." They were to eat the whole lamb, with the head, the legs, and the purtenance thereof; and so we are to feed on the whole of Christ. We need His head for our thoughts. "We have the mind of Christ." We need His legs for our walk; and the purtenance thereof covers everything that pertains to our life, and so there is nothing but Christ covers, supplies, fills. They were to leave none of it until the morning, and so there is nothing in Jesus that we can afford to leave unappropriated. He wants to fill all our life, to satisfy all our being, and to lead each one of us into the very fullness of union with Him in every particular. Let us take our sacrificial feast. It is not merely food; it is a feast. God does not merely supply all our necessities. He gives us abundance, wine upon the lees, fatness full of marrow, overflowing and boundless grace and bless-ing. So let us keep this sacred feast.

They were not to eat of it raw, but cooked with fire; and so the Holy Ghost must prepare Christ for us and make Him to be suitable nourishment. He only can; and He loves to minister Jesus to the hungry and thirsty heart, to take His fullness and feed it into us, until every part of our being is sweetly satisfied and strengthened by the living bread. And they were to eat together this feast. It was not a solitary meal. It is not possible for you or me to take Christ alone in all His fullness. It is with all saints that we enter into the height and depth and breadth of the love of Christ which passeth knowledge. The more narrow and isolated you are in your

Christian life, the less full and rich it will be; and the larger your heart, and the fuller your fellowship in Him, the more of Him will you enjoy. If their family was not big enough, they were to take in the stranger; and so God wants some of us to enlarge our circle of love, to unite our hearts with others in the full fellowship of holy love, fitly framed together to grow up into all the maturity of our Christian life.

There were some bitter herbs in this feast, but they only added zest to the sacred meal; even as our trials are turned into blessings, and become the bitter sweet of life when truly sanctified by the Holy Ghost to a loving, obedient heart.

III. THE LEAVEN.

This represents the element of corruption, fermentation, impurity. Therefore we are to purge out the old leaven that we may be a new lump, because we are unleavened. The leaven represents all that which is earthly and sinful; and we may know the leaven by its effects. That which produces the ferment of earthly passion, agitation, and unrest, selfish and unholy desire, rebellion against God, disobedience and sin, is leaven. There are two leavens. There is the old leaven. It is just the natural life which God wants laid down, and then taken up in His pure and heavenly life. And then there is a worst leaven, the leaven of malice and wickedness. All this must be purged out.

The purging is sometimes severe, for the evil is obstinate. As we have already said, the Jewish father searches the house with lighted candle to see if there is a crumb of leaven, and having done so, he solemnly pronounces the house to be clean. So with the word of God, we are to pass through the chambers of our heart, and having found any evil thing, cast it out, lay it down at the feet of Christ, and under the blood, and when we can find nothing that our heart can condemn us for, we are to rest, we are to pronounce the house clean, the lump unleavened, and hear the Master say to our peaceful heart, "Now are ye clean through the word that I have spoken unto you, abide in me, and I in you."

God does not want us to be in continual unrest and self-reproof; but in quietness and confidence to trust Him to keep us pure and holy. The enemy will love to sit upon us in judgment, and to have us to help him; but this is not promotive of holiness any more than the opening up of the grave, and the upturning of the bones of the dead could be promotive of health. Let us walk in innocency of heart, believing that we please God, and sweetly resting in His love. We cannot purge out the old leaven, but we can give it to Christ, and He will cleanse us by His own precious blood and Holy Spirit. And having yielded up to Him, we must believe that He does cleanse us, and walk in simple faith and self-forgetfulness, with holy vigilance, and yet with holy confidence in His leading and keeping grace and power.

IV. THE BREAD.

"The unleavened bread of sincerity and truth." Not only are we to be ourselves unleavened, but our daily bread must be unleavened. We cannot feed upon mixed food. The cause of weakness and suffering in most cases is that we feed so much upon earthly diet and forbidden bread. Sincerity literally means singleness, and truth suggests the idea of God's word, which is indeed our daily food. As we feed upon it unmixed with the exciting thoughts of man, we shall be fed and nourished in all godliness and sincerity, and shall grow in grace and in the knowledge of our Lord and Saviour Jesus Christ.

V. THE JOURNEY.

They were to eat their passover in haste, with loins girded, and shoes on their feet, and staves in their hands. They were on their way farther to their full inheritance; and so we go forth from the passover to all the fullness of our Father's will, and our future inheritance. Let our loins be girded for service. Let our feet be shod for our holy race. Let our hands hold the hand of promise. Let our vision be set firmly toward His coming, and all His holy will, and thus covered with His blood, and feeding upon His flesh, separated from all evil, and pressing on behind the pillar of cloud that leads our way, let us walk as strangers and pilgrims upon earth, looking and hastening unto the coming of our Lord, and preparing for it by lives of holy service and consecration.

CHAPTER VII.

CHRIST OUR PROPHET.

"A prophet shall the Lord your God raise up unto you of your brethren, like unto me; him shall ye hear." Acts vii: 37.

THE Hebrew prophets were the noblest class of men in ancient Israel. The priests were not always pure and true to God, for even the sons of Aaron brought dishonor upon themselves in the first generation; and the kings with few exceptions were unfaithful and unholy in the influence of their lives. The very best of them, David, Jehoshaphat, Hezekiah, and Josiah, were marked by the strongest imperfections, and many of them were blots upon the history of their country; but the prophets of Israel were always true, from Moses, the first glorious leader and teacher of God's inheritance, to John the Baptist, who closed the ancient dispensation, and ushered in the new. They

were all types of the great Prophet, whom
Stephen announces as their divine successor,
and the great Apostle and Prophet of our
profession, Jesus Christ. Let us look at His
prophetic office as it is illustrated by their
functions and their lives.

I. THE FUNCTIONS OF OUR GREAT PROPHET.

1. In general, the ancient prophet was the
messenger of God to the people, and the representative of His will concerning them. So
Jesus Christ to us is the messenger of Jehovah, the Word of God, the voice of divine
authority and divine love, who brings to us
God's will, and reveals to us His plan of salvation and life.

2. More particularly He is our teacher,
leading us into all the truth, and building us
up in our faith and life. It is He who gives
us the first ray of light that dawns upon the
darkness of the natural heart. It is He who
shows to us ourselves and Himself, and enables us to trust Him as our Saviour. It is
He who opens our inner eyes to see the light

that streams from heaven through the Word. It is He who shows to us the deeper truths of Christian life, our Sanctifier, our Life, our Healer, our help in every time of need. It is He, who as fast as we believe, enlarges our vision, our hope, our desire, our knowledge, our faith, and shows us the King in His beauty, and the land that is afar off. It is He who anoints our eyes with eye-salve that we may see, and then opens to us the light which we are able to receive. It is He who makes the truth not only light but life, and enables us to appropriate it, to believe it, to feed upon it, to be strengthened and quickened and sanctified by it. He is our wonderful Counselor, our unerring Teacher, our Faithful Prophet.

3. As our Prophet He guides us in perplexity, and shows us the way we should go. He not only gives us truth, but light upon our path. "He that followeth me shall not walk in darkness, but shall have the light of life." The ancient prophets were the counselors of the king and the nations in hours

of perplexity. Nathan came to David with the Lord's word concerning his important acts. Elisha was the counselor of the king. Samuel was the guide of Israel. Jesus is our leader and guide. When He putteth us forth, He goeth before us, and the sheep follow Him, for they know His voice. He will not let us err. "He will lead us in a straight way, wherein we shall not stumble," and He will stay with us nearest of all in the dark perplexities and crises of life.

4. As our Prophet He unfolds the vision of the future, showing us His plan concerning the world and the church thus especially His own personal coming, and preparing us to work for Him in intelligent hope and co-operation, and showing us as much of His plan for His own life as we need to know to inspire us with courage and enable us to meet with intelligence the duties and claims of life; whispering to our hearts the assurance of His answer to our prayers; leading out our new hopes in holy aspirations for service and blessing, and giving us

glimpses of the great and mighty things He would have us to aspire to and expect from Him.

5. As our Prophet He is the great wonder worker, for the prophet of old not only brought the message of God, but accredited it by signs and wonders, proving as Moses, Elijah and Elisha, by their supernatural working, that their message was indeed divine. So our Lord Jesus Christ, our own dear Prophet, brings us not only words, but deeds; fulfills what He commands, and ever seals His message to us by His own omnipotent and blessed working.

II. ILLUSTRATIONS OF CHRIST'S PROPHETIC WORK FROM THE LIVES OF THE ANCIENT PROPHETS.

1. In Moses we behold the first type of our great prophet. Born of the oppressed race, he was one of themselves, and could come near to their hearts in deepest sympathy. So Christ is a brother born of our flesh and blood, and further, a brother born for adver-

sity. To them He was the revealer of God's purpose of deliverance and redemption, and he led them out of Egypt into their covenant with Jehovah. So Christ, our great Prophet, reveals to us the great redemption, and leads us into it. He was the revealer to them of the law of God and the gospel, as unfolded in the wondrous Tabernacle and types; and so Jesus Christ is our teacher, not only of moral and spiritual truth, but especially of salvation, that glorious salvation of which the ancient Tabernacle was the wondrous type. Above all else, He was their devoted, faithful and unwavering Friend, utterly true to their interests amid the great discouragement and provocation, and never failing them even when they failed Him and proved wholly unfaithful to their God.

How often they disappointed Him and provoked their God, but never once did He falter in His faithful love. How often did they speak against Moses and Jehovah, and murmured in the wilderness, but He ever met them with new light and deliverance. And even when Jehovah seemed for a moment about to reject them and offered Moses a new inheritance of his own if he would give them up, Moses refused, and offered himself a sacrifice for the people he loved, crying, "Yet now, Lord, forgive their iniquity, and if not, blot me, I pray thee, out of thy book."

And yet again, when a more terrible crisis came, and they refused to enter the land of promise, and were driven back into the wilderness for forty years to perish in their unbelief, Moses did not leave them, but went back with them every step of the way, clinging to his unworthy children with more than a mother's love, until once more he brought them to the borders of their inheritance which he lost through their provocation.

Beautiful type of the more gracious, tender, faithful Prophet whom we follow! How often we grieve Him, and how faithfully He loves us and keeps us: "for He will never leave us, nor forsake us," until He shall have accomplished all His gracious will for all of us! More than the love of Moses is the love of Jesus! How we have proved that love already! We can trust it still, for He hath said, "the mountains shall depart, and the hills shall be removed; but my kindness shall not depart from thee; neither shall the covenant of my peace be removed, saith the Lord that hath mercy upon thee."

2. Or shall we look at Samuel, the great reformer, the prophet of Israel's return to God from the dark and long apostasy under the-judges, when for four hundred years the light of God's covenant presence was almost extinguished; the prophet who established the whole school of Hebrew prophets, and so shaped and formed out of the chaos of sin and wretchedness amid which he was born, the elements of unity, strength and stability in the kingdom of David, which he left as his heritage to Israel, and which were far more the work of his life than even of David's own faith and fidelity to God. Samuel,

the faithful friend of weak and inconstant Israel, expressed his noble spirit in the words which he said to them on one occasion, "God forbid that I should sin against the Lord in ceasing to pray for you; but I will teach you the right way and the good way." Samuel was the type of Jesus, the prophet of the poor backslider, the Christ that restored Peter and Thomas, and that still tenderly and faithfully awaits to welcome back the wanderer to His bosom again. How tenderly He loves the contrite heart! How graciously He restores the child! How sweetly He forgives! How mightily He keeps! How faithfully He loves! How perfectly He heals our backslidings, and becomes "the dew upon Israel, and reviving us as the corn, and causing us to grow as the vine, our smell as Lebanon," and leading us on and up until we are established, strengthened and built up, and settled, and become like Israel of old, His own royal kingdom and throne.

3. Elijah tells us of the great prophet of reproof and correction, the loving Teacher

who has sometimes to show us our faults, and to chasten us for them in tender love. Elijah was the faithful reprover of sin, and represented the judicial element in God. So our great Prophet has often to correct His people, and show them their faults and lead them from the error of their ways by His heart-searching discipline. But He is a better reprover than Elijah; for there is no better evidence than the life of Elijah himself of the failure of even that greatest of prophets, and the tender faithfulness of the true Prophet who dealt with him as He does with us. Would we see the true spirit of Jesus our Prophet? Let us look at the God of Elijah, as the poor broken prophet lies under the juniper tree, a fugitive and a failure after the highest triumph of his glorious life. How gently God deals with him! He first rests him with sleep, and then feeds him by angel hands, then sends him alone to Horeb, and asks him, "What doest thou here, Elijah?" True He speaks with the earthquake, the whirlwind and the fire, but He ends with the still, small voice. The last message is a restoration of his commission, and a renewal of his call to service as He sends him forth to anoint Jehu, Hazael and Elisha for the work that yet remains to be done. So gently yet faithfully does our dear Prophet teach us; not crushing the spirit that would fail before Him or the souls that He has made, but tenderly leading us into all His light, and then making the very best of us, notwithstanding our worst failures. Let us never doubt our faithful Christ, our wonderful Counselor, our mighty God, our everlasting Father, our Prince of Peace.

4. The most beautiful prophetic life of the Old Testament was that of Elisha, and he is a perfect type of Jesus Christ, our Prophet. Elijah represented the law; Elisha, the gospel; Elijah, the discipline of judgment; Elisha, the salvation of grace. Elijah was the thunderbolt and lightning; Elisha, the sunshine and light. Elijah was the woodman's axe and fire; Elisha, the husbandman with his seed and watering-pot, with fields of green and har-

vests of golden grain. Elisha's is the ministry of love—the ministry of Jesus. He begins by healing the barren land and the water by sprinkling salt in its fountains. Like the great Prophet who does not blame the outflowing of our lives so much, but rather goes to the fountain-head and heals the source of our thoughts, motives and actions by the touch of His mighty love.

Look at him again as he meets the baffled kings of Judah, Israel and Edom in the valley of dearth and famine; and instead of blaming them for their mistake, gently interposes for their deliverance, commands the valley to be filled with ditches, claims from heaven the floods of water to fill all the mighty spaces, and overflow in blessing for the perishing armies. So our great Prophet comes to us in the calamities that we have brought upon ourselves, and delivers us, and then gently leads us to greater blessings. Look at him again as the poor widow appeals to him for help against the creditors who are about to seize upon her sons for her debts.

"What hast thou in the house?" is all he asks, and then commands the pot of oil to be brought forth and poured into all the empty vessels she can find or borrow, until they are all filled to overflowing, and she is rich with a harvest of faith; and then he bids her sell the oil, pay her debts, and live upon the rest.

So our great Prophet meets us in every emergency by showing us that we have within our house the one remedy for everything that tries us. The little pot of oil, the Holy Spirit, so faint it may be in His manifested presence that it seems less than the little finger of our hand; but that is the little finger of God, and back of it lies all His omnipotence, wisdom and love, and all we have to do is to take that Holy Spirit and pour it into every vessel of need, both for ourselves and others, and lo! the vessels overflow and the blessings only cease when we cease to make room and to pour out.

Look at him again as the sons of the prophet lose their borrowed axe in the river

Jordan, where they had been cutting wood for their house, and the axe had slipped from the handle to the bottom of the river. Instantly he orders a branch or handle to be dropped into the river, and lo! immediately the axe rises to the surface, and the lost implement is recovered by the hands of the young men. So our great Prophet is equal to the smallest as well as the largest emergencies. We, too, lose our axe sometimes —our power for service, our victory over temptation, our peace and joy, our consciousness of Christ's presence; but there is a piece of wood—the pilgrim's staff, the sacred promise—that we can ever find equal to the emergency, and, as we cast it into the water, lo! our blessing will rise to meet it, our lost axe will come back to us; the very laws of nature may be suspended, the iron can swim again, the thing that was heavier than lead can rise with buoyant wings, the heavy heart can mount above and sing and trust with new power and victory, and we can praise Him whose faithful love has turned darkness into day and sorrow into joy.

Or look again at his triumph over his enemies.   The armies of Syria surrounded him
and his servant, and the servant gives a cry
of despair, "Alas! my master," as he sees no
possible way of escape.   All that Elisha asks
is that the eyes of his servant may be
opened, and lo! on the mountain round about
there are armies of angelic horses and char-
iots and soldiers, and instantly their fears
are calmed, and they know that all is well.
So, beloved, our great Prophet can show us,
though every avenue of escape be shut off,
that there is ever an upper way that carries
us above our foes, and a superior host that
has the advantage of position over all our
foes.   But that is not all.   He then asks the
Lord to blind the soldiers, and so he goes
down to them without a fear, and leads
them all the way to the city of Samaria.   It
is indeed a triumph as amusing as it is sublime.   When they reach the city the king is
so delighted to have his enemies in his power
that he wants to slay them.   Elisha treats
the proposal as absurd, and orders that a

magnificent banquet be prepared for them;
and so they feed them and feast them until
the men are astounded, paralyzed with wonder and dismay at the treatment they have
received, and when all is over, they are sent
back to their own land to tell how easily the
prophet of Israel has defeated them without
a blow, except from the hand of love. We
need hardly wonder when it is added, that
the bands of the Syrians came no more unto
the land of Israel. And so our great Prophet
teaches us to triumph over our foes by the
weapons of heavenly love, that the surest
way to kill our enemies is by kindness, to
consume them by the coals of fire of loving
deeds and words and recompenses.

Such is the great and gracious Prophet
that is willing to walk by our side, that
is willing to dwell in our heart of hearts,
to be our wisdom, our guide. Happy they
that walk in His fellowship and in His love!
For them no emergency can be extreme, no
situation can be desperate, no adversary can
be formidable. No purpose formed from

above can fail. Blessed Prophet, thou art ours! Help us to abide in thee, and follow thee evermore!

5. We might speak of Isaiah, the prophet of high and holy teaching, as the type of Him who leads us into the high and loftiest heights of heavenly truth and life, where the seraphim veil their faces and feet with their wings, and exclaim, "Holy! Holy! Holy! is the Lord God of hosts, the whole earth is full of His glory;" where faith mounts up on high to see "the king in His beauty, and the land that is far off;" where peace nestles under the shadow of the Rock of Ages; where hope looks out upon His coming, and sings "The ransomed of the Lord shall return and come to Zion with songs, and everlasting joy upon their heads; they shall obtain joy and gladness, and sorrow and sighing shall flee away." Or again, "The sun shall no more go down; neither shall the moon withdraw itself; for the Lord shall be thy everlasting light, and the days of thy mourning shall be ended." Or holy

service waits His power and bidding, and exclaims, "He wakeneth me morning by morning, as one that has been instructed that I may know how to speak a word in season to him that is weary;" or, going forth to do His bidding, sing, "How beautiful upon the mountain are the feet of Him that bringeth good tidings, that publisheth peace; that bringeth good tidings of joy; that publisheth salvation; that saith unto Zion, Thy God reigneth!" Or prayer reaches out in the name of Jesus, with mighty faith, and obeys the great injunction, "Ask me of things concerning my sons, and concerning the work of my hands command ye me." Or holy gladness lifts up its voice and sings, "Therefore with joy shall ye draw water out of the wells of salvation. Cry out and shout, thou inhabitant of Zion: for great is the Holy One of Israel in the midst of thee." So still our Prophet speaks to us, and teaches us and leads us as we abide in Him.

5. We might speak of Daniel, the prophet of the future, as the type of Him who un-

folds to us the vision of His coming, and as much of His will for us as it is best for us to know or hope for, for Jesus also shows to us the things to come, and leads us into the life of hope as well as of faith and love.

Such is our glorious Prophet. Is He not dearer to us to day? Shall we not trust Him more fully, follow Him more closely, listen to Him more lovingly and obediently, and seek to send abroad His glorious truth among all nations, until the Prophet and the Priest shall have become the King of Kings and reign from shore to shore.

CHAPTER VIII.

MAKING DAVID KING.

"All these were of one heart to make David king."
1 Chron. xii: 38.

IN ONE of the chapels of Oxford University there is a beautiful stained glass window, the exterior of which is decorated with sacred pictures from the Old Testament, the interior with corresponding pictures from the New, so that, when the sunlight falls upon the window, the two pictures are blended, and an observer, standing inside of the cathedral, beholds the soft evening light falling upon the picture of Mount Moriah and Abraham's sacrifice of his son Isaac, and at the same time upon the cross of Calvary, which interprets the Old Testament type; or again, perhaps, upon the brazen serpent as it blends with the great sacrifice of the Son of Man. Beautifully does this illustrate the connection between the Old Testament and the New, and the glorious fact that all the scenes of the ancient Scriptures are but figures, whose full meaning must be learned in the light of the gospel and the life and death of Jesus Christ!

Of all the Old Testament types of Christ, none is more remarkable than David—born in Bethlehem, as Jesus was, a simple shepherd foreshadowing the great Shepherd, a sufferer and an exile like the Man of Sorrows, he at length became king, and is pre-eminently the type of Christ as our great King and Lord. In this respect he differed from Solomon, his son. Both of them are types of our coming King, but Solomon is the type rather of the kingdom after it shall have become established in peace and righteousness. David, on the contrary, foreshadows the King of Kings in the years and centuries of His rejection by the world, and as He slowly conquers His kingdom and wins the crown which He is to wear with His saints through the ages of glory.

This is His position to-day. Like David He has been anointed, and been proclaimed the King of the church and the nations, but like David He is rejected by the great majority of mankind, and a counterfeit king usurps the throne, of whom Saul was the type. The world to-day is not subject to the will of God and the sceptre of Jesus, and never will be until He comes a second time. Even the church has refused, in large measure, to be subject to her King, and has allowed the spirit of the world to control and contaminate her. But the true David has still His loyal friends and followers, although, like the followers of David in his exile, they are often the humblest of men and yet more and more will be the very outcasts of the world, but their connection with David made them illustrious, and to serve Jesus is enough to dignify and glorify any human name.

This is the great object of our gathering at this time, and this is the great business of all true Christians to-day—to make Christ King. Let us first look at the way in which this may be accomplished, and secondly, at the character of the men on whom He depends to accomplish it, as illustrated in the picture of these ancient worthies who followed the fortunes of David and won for him his crown.

I.

1. Each of us can give Christ the kingdom of our own heart; and He will not use us to establish His kingdom in the world until He occupies the throne of our entire being, and becomes the King of our affections, our motives and our will, and all our heart. This must be done by the full surrender of love— a love that supremely gives Him the highest place, and makes Him our all in all. The ancient Pantheon offered a niche to the Christians for the image of Jesus, but they answered, "Our God must reign alone; we can have but one king, and Christ must be the sovereign of all our hearts." He is preparing to-day a people for His glory, and

this is to be the test, that they follow the Lamb whithersoever He goeth, and give Him the bridal love which displaces every other which could for a moment hinder His supremacy. Beloved, have we given Christ all our heart, and do we gladly do it now; for the answer of your consciousness is the best test of your consecration.

2. You can take Christ as the King of your life by giving Him your difficulties and adversaries to overcome, and permitting Him to subdue all His enemies and yours, and reign the Lord of all. Everything that comes up in your life is but another opportunity of giving Him a larger and richer crown. It is too strong for you, but not for Him. Your land of promise is not a luxurious inheritance of self-indulgent ease, but a battle-field of countless foes, and ever harder, nobler triumphs. Every confederacy of hostile kings that comes up to meet you, is but another challenge to prove the might of your great Captain and all-conquering King, and, instead of shrinking and com-

plaining that the conflict is so hard and the foes so mighty and so many, you should recognize them as His foes rather than yours, and hand them over to Him for still more glorious victories. "It was of the Lord that those kings should have come against Joshua with the intent that they might be utterly destroyed." Every son of Anak that marched out against the armies of Israel was sent forth at God's command, not to destroy Israel, but to meet their own destruction; and but for the battle there could never have been the annihilation of the foe, and so he says to us, "In nothing terrify your actions, which is to them an evident token of perdition, but to you of salvation and that of God." There is nothing ever comes up in your life but Christ anticipated it long ago, has been prepared for it from the beginning, and, if you will let Him, will carry you through it in glorious victory. This is the meaning of His kingdom; He is thus winning for you and Himself a mutual crown. Will you, beloved, exalt Him over all your

difficulties and trials, and crown Him Lord
of all ?

3. We can make Christ King by laboring
for the evangelization of the world, and the
spread of His glorious truth and work. We
can win for Him the crown of many hearts,
and thus hasten His glorious coming.

There are two ways especially in which
this can be done. The first is in calling cut
His bride even from the church ; not neces-
sarily in the sense of separating them from
the communion of the church, but rather in
the sense of separating them unto Him in
entire consecration. He is preparing for
Himself a bride, not consisting of mere pro-
fessors, but of those who are wholly His,
separated from the world and sin, robed in
the whitest garments of His perfect righteousness, and wedded in affection to Him
alone as their Bridegroom and Lord.

And then we can all accomplish this by
spreading the gospel among the unsaved,
and sending it out especially to the heathen
world. The great call of the Master to-day

is to the evangelization of the nations; and
when this has been accomplished, there will
be no barrier in the way of His immediate
return. Are we thus laboring to make Christ
King, spreading His glorious truth, and calling all nations to prepare for His millennial
reign? This is the real purpose of God for
His church to-day ; not so much to build up
great and permanent institutions, as to be a
messenger of the glad tidings, and to publish
among the nations the glorious news that
the King is about to come.

Napoleon, in his hour of pride, refused to
receive a crown from human hands, but,
taking in his own fingers the royal diadem,
and placing it upon his brow, he exclaimed,
"These hands have won; these hands alone
shall give the crown of empire." But the
Lord Jesus desires to receive His crown
from those who love Him, and honors us
with the great privilege of winning it for
Him and laying it at His dear feet. The
Lord help us to hasten His kingdom, and to
add to the glory of His many crowns.

II. WHO ARE THEY ON WHOM HE RELIES TO MAKE HIM KING?

1. They had all been unhappy, helpless, and indeed, we might say, worthless men, for we read that whosoever was in debt or in any kind of trouble resorted to David in the cave of Adullam, and David made them one of His mighty men. Before they came to him they were the outlaws of society, but the moment they touched David they became ennobled, and afterwards were raised to be his princes and the officers of the kingdom. Even so we, whom Christ has chosen as His friends and fellow-workers, are by nature poor, unworthy sinners, with nothing to recommend us but simply this —that we have followed Jesus, and that He has touched us with His royal hand; and this is enough to make us glorious and illustrions. Sinners by nature and practice we have been washed in His precious blood, and our love to Him is accepted as better than royal blood, and by-and-by He will say to us, "Ye are they which have continued with me

in my temptations. And I appoint unto you a kingdom, as my Father has appointed unto me, that ye may eat and drink at my table in my kingdom, and sit on thrones, judging the twelve tribes of Israel."

2. In the description of the respective tribes that came up to make David King, we read of the Benjamites (1 Chronicles xii: 2), that "They were armed with bows, and could use both the right hand and the left in hurling stones and shooting arrows out of a bow." They were two-handed men, *i. e.*, all their power was given to their master, and they were ready, not only in season, but out of season, for service and warfare. So Christ would have His true soldiers not only speak out of a pulpit, or to read from a manuscript, but ever prepared to speak a word of warning, or comfort, or salvation, as opportunity requires.

3. They were armed men (verse 8). They "could handle shield and buckler; whose faces were like the faces of lions, and were as swift as the roes upon the mountains."

There is a difference between a shield and a buckler. A shield is something that you hold yourself, but a buckler is something that is fastened upon the arm, and that cannot be lost. There is a kind of faith that we cling to, and there is a faith that holds us, and that we cannot lose—even the faith of God—like the buckler on the arm which we retain in the heat of battle, and which even the dying warrior still holds above his breast. This is the faith that Christ would have us receive, and in which He would have us conquer.

4. They were courageous men; they feared no danger (verse 15). "These are they that went over Jordan in the first month, when it had overflown all its banks, and they put to flight all them of the valleys, both toward the east and toward the west." They had a hard test. As they approached the Jordan there were enemies upon the east, but they scattered them like the smoke before the wind. Next, the Jordan had flooded its banks and could not be forded, but they

sprang into the flood and swam across, fearing neither flood nor foe. And when they reached the farther shore, still the enemy stood facing them along the banks, but they put them to flight. Perhaps they did not even wait for the battle, for men so brave were not likely to meet a formidable resistance. And when we press through the tides of opposition and the hosts of hell, we shall find our enemies still encamped before us, and each battle will be on the verge of a greater victory still to come.

5. They were true-hearted men (verses 17, 18). " And David went out to meet them, and answered and said unto them, If ye be come peaceably unto me to help me, mine heart shall be knit unto you; but if ye come to betray me to mine enemies, seeing there is no wrong in mine hands, the God of our fathers look thereon and rebuke it. Then the Spirit came upon Amasai, who was chief of the captains, and he said, ' Thine are we, David, and on thy side, thou son of Jesse; peace, peace be unto thee, and peace be to

thine helpers, for thy God helpeth thee.'"
So Christ wants loyal friends: loyal not only
to Him, but loyal to His people, too. Their
cry was not only, peace be unto thee, but
peace be to thy helpers.

6. Next, they were wise men (verse 32).
"And of the children of Issachar, which
were men that had understanding of the
times to know what Israel ought to do."
And so our King wants wise men to-day;
men that do not waste their strength in mis-
guided efforts, men that are not fighting
over old issues long since obsolete, or beat-
ing the air with mere speculations and theo-
ries that have no practical bearing, men of
to-day that understand the Lord's meaning for our times and catch His thought for
their generation, and are living for the work
of the present hour. Such men, like the men
of Issachar, have all their brethren at their
command, and exert the sacred influences
which control their minds and make them
leaders of the great hosts of God.

7. They were men that could keep rank

(verse 33). That is, they were adjustable and congenial men, who could work in co-operation with others; not narrow, bigoted and impracticable people, with whom nobody could work, as Christians sometimes are, but large-hearted, loving, humble workers, who knew their places, who took any place, who were not afraid to take the lowest place, who could obey orders as well as give them, who could walk in fellowship with other soldiers, who could keep step with other soldiers and maintain the unbroken rank in the host of God. God give us this Spirit! The nearer we are to God the less angular we will be, and the easier it will be to work with us.

8. Again, they were single-hearted men (verse 33). "They were not of double heart." Their whole heart was with David. Their whole interest was invested in his kingdom. Their whole being was given to his honor and advancement. And so we cannot be true soldiers for Christ unless we have given Him all our heart; and nothing can separate us from Him when we are utterly devoted

to His honor and interest, every other attachment and every other interest being subject to His highest will and glory, and eternally linked with His kingdom. We cannot have our heart in the world that has no interest in Him and on things that must perish, but every part of our being is invested in His coming and His glory.

This is also the meaning of the perfect heart referred to in verse 38. God give us such a spirit in the blessed work of hastening the coming of our blessed Lord!

Beloved, we are passing through the days of David's suffering and humiliation. He is not yet upon the throne of this world, although He has the right to reign, and a sure degree has been passed in heaven, "I have set my King upon my holy hill of Zion." But He is now in the days of His obscurity, and the badge of His service is a cross and a crown. He is passing through the world and picking out His future princes, and testing them by their loyal devotion to His person and will. Oh, that we all may be true in these days, and honored with a part of the glory in that day!

It is said that the great Ivan of Russia used to love to go among his people in disguise and test them. One night he went through the suburbs of his capital, and knocked at many lowly cabins as a poor, wandering tramp, asking for a night's lodging and a crust of bread. He was refused from door to door, until at last he came to a humble cabin, where a poor man was attending his wife and new-born babe. He opened the door at the knock of the wanderer, kindly invited him in, treated him with courtesy and attention, gave him a rude bed and a humble supper, and bade him goodnight with great kindness. The emperor lay, sleeping little and thinking much, and in the early morning he took his leave amid many thanks. Late in the afternoon the royal chariot drove to the door and halted. The poor man fled to the gate in great alarm, prostrated himself at the feet of his emperor, and asked him if he had committed any crime to cause his displeasure. The emperor assured him it was all right, and then added, "I have simply come to thank you for your kindness to your emperor last night. He came in the disguise of a begger to test your love, and now he comes as your sovereign to reward your loyalty. This bag of gold is for your new-born child. As he grows up I will adopt him as my child, and will give him a place of high and honorable service in the empire, and if I can be of any service to you and yours, command your emperor."

So Christ is passing by to-day. So He is coming soon. The Lord help us to know Him and receive Him in His lowliness, and may ours be the joy in that day of receiving His smile and recognition in the midst of a dissolving world and a despairing multitude!

CHAPTER IX.

CHRIST OUR HEAD.

"And he is the head of the body, the church : who is the beginning, the firstborn from the dead; that in all things he might have the preeminence. For it pleased the Father that in him should all fullness dwell." Col. i: 18, 19.

THE human body is the paragon and crown of the material universe. It was the last thing that God ever created, and so satisfied was He with His glorious work that He chose this wondrous and beautiful temple for His own abode, and has made the form of man forevermore the embodiment of His own eternal Son. The fact that Jesus Christ is incarnate in a body like our own, has placed humanity on the pinnacle of creation and the throne of God. Forever and forever a wondering universe will come to behold their God, and will see Him in a form like yours and mine. It is little wonder, therefore, that this exquisite workmanship of God should be worthy of the honor and dignity conferred upon it, and should show in all its structures the works of infinite wisdom, power and love. Even David, long before the study of physiology had revealed the wonders of the human frame, could say, "I will praise thee, for I am fearfully and wonderfully made." How much more profound the wonder and praise that should fill our hearts as the progress of human knowledge enables us better to understand the exquisite and infinite skill displayed in the creation of a single member of our body!

Perhaps the most striking evidence of Christianity ever presented in Christian literature was the Bridgewater treatise on the human hand, showing the delicate mechanism of the hundreds of bones, nerves, vessels, and the varied and perfect functions of the various parts of e en that little member. How much more delicate and perfect the structure of the human brain and the relation of the head to all the physical organism of the vital functions! This is the figure which the apostle uses to express the relation of Jesus Christ to His people and their mutual relationship to Him as the body of Christ. May His Spirit enable us to apply the beautiful figure in such a way that we shall be drawn closer to our living Head and to one another in Him!

I. THE HEAD.

1. In the human body the head is the seat of will and authority, and the body is obedient to its volitions, and these commands are so simple and so instructive that the body obeys without an effort. It is perfectly natural to follow the wishes of the head, so the Lord Jesus Christ our living Head, is the true Lord and sovereign of His people's lives, and it is the place of their bodies to be instinctively obedient to His every wish. If He is indeed our Head, it will be our second nature to do His bidding. Indeed, no other part of the body has any power to will, and none of Christ's children should have any

will apart from their Master's. There is a
great difference between being guided by
your own head or somebody else's. If Christ
is not your living Head you will not want
His `authority and government. Before,
therefore, we can truly obey Him we must
fully receive Him and so be united with Him
that His interests are ours, and His will is
just the expression of our inmost being.
Beloved, is Christ our recognized and honored Head, and is our life a glad and constant
obedience to His every wish and prompting?

2. In the human body the head is the
source and seat of life, and so the Lord Jesūs
is the source of His people's life. There is
no life apart from the head, and we have
none apart from Him. Our regeneration
comes through the quickening power of His
life, our sanctification is His indwelling in us.
Our physical life may be made manifest in
the flesh. We are dependent upon Him for
our fruit, for our joy, for our love, for all
our spiritual grace and experiences, and He
loves to impart His life to us and fill us more

abundantly if we will but receive it. We are not held responsible for our own life. We are not expected to manufacture either faith or love, but to receive from Him life and love, and the grace that He is ever longing to impart.

3. The head is the source of sensation. All feeling comes from the brain, and resides in it. When you hurt your hand it is not your hand that feels, but your head, although it seems to be in your members. Beautiful parable of the sympathy of our living Head! Every sorrow and pain we feel is instinctively telegraphed to Him, and touches His living heart to the quick, "For we have not an high priest who is not able to be touched with the feeling of our infirmities." When Paul was outraging the saints of God, and compelling them to blaspheme the name of Jesus under penalty of death, the voice of the Master called to Him from heaven, "Saul, Saul, why persecutest thou me?" He was hurting, not others, but the Master's heart. The heavenly head was suffering for the

earthly members. The hurt hand was communicating its pain to the head in heaven. How quickly the head sends relief to the suffering hand or foot! Have you ever noticed when you receive a blow or are pierced with a thorn, how quickly all the blood in the body rushes to the injured place, and it flushes with the crimson tide? It simply means that the brain has become concerned for the suffering member, and has ordered all the resources of the system on duty, and every drop of blood in the body is coursing to the sore place to give it a touch of relief. What you call an inflammation is just the effort of nature through increased circulation to lave away the intruding pain and stimulate and quicken the system to throw it off.

So Christ is ever nearest the sad heart, the tempted child, the wandering one, and all the resources of His grace are at our service in every time of need.

When Margaret Wilson was standing tied to a stake on Solway Beach, for the tide to

come in and take her martyred life, they
placed an older saint farther down the beach
that little Margaret might see the saintly
woman die before her turn. should come;
and thus be dissuaded by terror from her
bold testimony to Jesus, but as the cruel
waves leaped on Margaret McLaughlin and
trampled out her life, and the rough soldier
by Margaret Wilson's side asked, hoping to
turn her back from her purpose even at the
last, "What do you think of that?" she
meekly answered, "I think I see Christ in
one of His members suffering there." How
beautiful! How true!

When the pressure seems intolerable, when
sorrow gnaws the heart, and Satan hurls his
arrows of flame into our quivering spirit,
when the world opposes us as it once did
Him, and flesh and heart are ready to faint
and fail, it is just Christ in one of His members suffering there, and the living Head
will not fail nor forget to help the suffering
member, and will also help us in the matter
of religious feeling. All sensation must

come from the brain, and so all spiritual
feeling must come from Christ. Let us not,
therefore, try to work up our feelings, but
keep close to Him, and the tides of His love
will flow into our consciousness and spiritual
sensibilities. The secret of joy and love simply lie in nearness to Jesus, and His joy and
love will spring within us from the Head.
The most artless and spontaneous life will
ever be the best. Oftentimes He may wish
us to be quiescent. Let us be acquiescent in
this, and when He rests in His love, let us
rest with Him, and when He rejoices over
us with singing, let us swell the chorus in
glad response, our hearts keeping time to
His, as the sand upon the ocean shore is wet
or dry as the ocean tide rises and falls in the
sea below.

4. The head is the seat of power, and so
Christ is His people's power. We are not
strong in ourselves; but He is our strength.
"All power is given unto me in heaven and
in earth, and lo I am with you always."
"Ye shall receive the power of the Holy

Ghost coming upon you." This, therefore, is the secret of effective service. You shall always feel the power which does not reside in you, but as you go forth obedient to the orders of the Head, the Head will follow up your obedient steps and render effectual your service. Christ never sends His people on any ministry without equipping them, sustaining them, and rendering their work effectual. Your usefulness does not depend upon natural gifts nor conditions, but upon your closeness to your Head.

A very humble Christian ever filled with Jesus will so speak, so look, so grasp your hand, so do the commonest things of life, that strange and everlasting forces will spring from the act and touch hearts on every side. A very small wire filled with electricity will make everybody conscious of strange power. The other day all the horses became greatly excited at a certain point of the street, and reared and plunged as they came near. The reason was that there was electricity in the ground. A wire had become detached and they knew the strange power was ready to upheave the pavement. They could have walked over the wire harmlessly had it been dead, but it was connected with the dynamo in yonder works, and drew all its strength from the headquarters. It is a glorious and mighty thing to stand among men and be conscious that you have the authority and power of the Almighty, and that He is charging your messages with a weight and responsibilty which will meet those men in the judgment, and which will move and influence their whole earthly life whether they hear or whether they forbear.

5. The head is the seat of thought, intelligence, judgment, direction, knowledge. So Christ is our wisdom, our guide, our mind. We need not think so much, or rather He will think in us His thoughts, if we suspend our judgment, and draw upon His glorious mind for our knowledge, our light, our views, our opinions and plans. It is not the business of the hand to be planning and thinking, but simply to go forward at the bidding of

the brain, and so He has said to us, "Take no anxious thought for the morrow. Your Heavenly Father knoweth that you have need of these things." "Casting all your care upon Him, for He careth for you."

5. The head is the seat of honor, glory, and beauty. It supports the lovely face. It crowns the glorious temple. It is borne aloft in dignity and majesty, and in all things has the pre-eminence. It wears the crown of royalty, or the wreath of beauty, and is the expression and embodiment of dignity and pre-eminence. So Jesus Christ is the glory of His people, the crowned Head of His church and the One to whom alone belong all dominion, praise and love for ever and ever. To Him, not to us, belongs the honor. He is our Head and our glory, and He forever shall receive the many crowns of all His dear ones whose joy it shall be to lay them at His feet, or heap them upon His head. All His richest blessings must lead us from them to Him. All His dearest children must be but links and channels to lift our hearts

to Him from whom comes all love and all loveliness in earth or heaven.

II. THE BODY.

The body is as necessary as the head. A bodiless head would be as abnormal as a headless body, and so our blessed Lord needs us as much as we need Him. He has separated Himself from His old place of absolute Deity, and chosen for His inheritance His people, and without them His life is incomplete. All the gifts that He has received from the Father need an outlet, and we are the channels through whom they find expression and development. His love to men, His purpose to redeem them, His grace and power can only reach them through our intervention, and when we are not at His bidding and open to His influence, He is paralyzed in His purpose and baffled in His designs, like a man whom we have known, whose brain was full of magnificent energy and purpose, and whose heart was throbbing with boundless love, but whose limbs were paralyzed, and whose hands were limp and dead, and his body refusing to perform the wishes of his brain and clogging and depressing him with its helplessness, his love all vain because of the want of harmony and the lack of correspondence between the body and the head.

Christ has been hindered for eighteen centuries by the paralyzed, disjointed, diseased condition of many members of His body, and the work accomplished by the church has been limited by the fact that to so great an extent the body has been diseased and enfeebled in many of its parts. Oh, what might not be realized in a few days for the accomplishment of redemption if the entire body of Christ, without an exception, were open to the love of the Head, and obedient to all His wishes and will. Pentecost would be repeated with a multiplication as vast as the difference between the one hundred and twenty millions of Christians to-day and the one hundred and twenty brethren in the upper room. There are a million times as many members in the body to-day as there were then, but the very number restrains the body all the more when they are not perfectly adjustable and responsive to the head. Will you remember, beloved, that Jesus needs you, and that even if you be the weakest and smallest member, you have the power by becoming diseased and inflamed to spread disease through the whole body, even as the smallest finger on your hand can paralyze your hand by simply getting sick and sore?

Three things especially are emphasized by the apostle in his beautiful teaching about the body of Christ, namely:

1. Its variety. "We have many members in one body, and all members have not the same office, so we being many are one body in Christ." In your body there are more than two hundred bones, and in your whole body there are thousands of constituent elements. Every one is necessary. The very diversity of those members is your strength. Members of the church of Christ

are not all alike.   The greater the diversity
the more their power.   Each of us has our
natural individuality, and this is the element
through which God moulds our spiritual life
and our life plans.   He has made each of us
for a certain place and service, and the very
things that constitute our personal identity
are the things He wants to use in us.

Sometimes our very eccentricities are elements of force when consecrated to God and
baptized with the Holy Ghost.   Sometimes
the very facts of your previous history, even
your sins and errors, become features which
God can utilize for His kingdom.   Do not,
therefore, criticise your peculiarities.   They
are the very things God wants, if they be
not defects.   Your very littleness may just
fit you for the place He wants you to fill.
In making up a body He sometimes wants a
finger only or a single hair.   Now if you
were a thumb, or a glowing eye, you would
be needless, because, you see, there are
enough of these already, and you are just
required to fit into your place and functions.

Do not criticise in others their idiosyncrasies, as you are pleased to call them, for in the body there are some curious members, and the apostle says that those that have least honor, to them God has given more abundant honor, and the time often comes when those obscure and uncongenial persons become, perhaps, the greatest blessings of your life, and draw you to them as the Lord Himself.

2. Unity. These diversities may all be blended and kept by a common band of love and life in Jesus. If completely united, the very diversity adds greatly to the scope and influence of the church of Christ. On the field of Gettysburg a little pool of blood was found, into which flowed five tiny streams, and when the men from whose wounds the life tides were issuing were found, they proved to be the sons of different races, so that in that little crimson pool the heart of a German, a Frenchman, an Irishman, a Negro and an American were all blending; and it had but one color and one

meaning, the love of country that was not afraid to die. If Christ's love is in our heart all differences become small. A creed will not unite us, a work will not unite us, a love, and a love only, can. Closeness to Jesus brings closeness to each other. The little birdlings that are always nestling against the mother's bosom are always pushing against each other, and if you and I determine to be nearer to Jesus, we shall never be far apart. A lack of unity in the body is fatal to health and power. An obstructive joint will bring rheumatism and paralysis. The reason to-day that the power of the Holy Ghost is so limited is because the interflow and the outway of the life of Christ are hindered by the divisions of Christianity, and still more by the lack of heart-oneness to Him.

3. Relationship. We owe to each other certain mutual obligations expressed by the phrase, " fitly joined together and compacted by that which every joint supplieth." While every member of the body sustains a rela-

tionship in some sense to every other, yet some are closer than others, and in those intimate relationships there must be perfect freedom, fellowship and holy activity. The joint and the socket must move together without friction. The least friction will produce inflammation, irritation, pain, disease, paralysis. God adjusts us to each other by His Providence and Spirit, and He will enable us to recognize our relationships, to meet them, and to fulfill them perfectly with holy wisdom and love. Each of us sustains many relationships, but the Holy Spirit in us will adjust us to each with a perfect freedom and delicacy, so that we shall love one another in Christ in the places where we belong, with a heart as free as heaven and as pure as Christ Himself. You shall have a boundless love for each of God's children, each in his place. You will love your family, your children, your friends, your brother in Christ, each in his or her place with perfect simplicity of heart, and yet without a jar in the various relationships, for if Christ is abiding in us He will adjust us to every relationship even as He Himself meets each of His members with the fullness of His heart, and yet the special adaptation of each one is what their situation requires.

The recognizing of our oneness with Christ will make us considerate of one another, and will give to our duty to each other a higher sacredness, inasmuch as it affects the whole body and the Head Himself. When you hinder or hurt a single brother, you hurt the whole body just the same as in your physical body a jar in one part will hinder. And not only so, you will come to recognize the necessity of being right with God, for otherwise you may hinder the entire work of Christ. It does not need for a man to be sick all over to be helpless. A single weak organ will render him helpless, and so, if you choose, you can, by becoming an irritation and an offense, arrest and obstruct all God's work to a certain extent. Of course, there is provision in the human body for getting rid of such a member, and sometimes the only thing is to cut it off; and so God has the same provision for His church, and He will separate you from His people if you are not willing to work with them in harmony and holiness. And yet excision always leaves a scar, and often a lack. The law of love and the desire of the Master is that we should be so true to Him and to each other that He can accomplish in us and through us His highest purposes of love and blessing. It will help us infinitely in our relationship with people to recognize them in Christ and not in themselves. Then our love to them may not be personal and selfish, but will be heavenly and holy. Then also we shall be enabled to love what naturally we could not even tolerate.

Oh, we little know the depths and heights of joy and power that lie hidden in recogniz- ing the mystery of the body of Christ, and Christ Himself in all His members! Then our service will be all unto Him, and a cup of cold water given to a disciple for Jesus' sake will bring a great reward, and some day the Master will say, "Ye did it unto me." Then also it will be found that the simplest and humblest services have been of the greatest value, even as the poor old widow in ancient Constantinople that could only sprinkle the grass upon the rough stones as they dragged them to the temple, is represented in the old legend as having her name inscribed on the front of the Cathedral in letters of gold traced by an angel's hand, "This house the widow Eudoxia built for God."

Then also will we know the exceeding joy of doing much of our work through others, and doing the rest almost unconsciously and impersonally until the day comes when He will trace each constituent, and give to each his proportionate reward. I am so glad to feel that in that day most of my work for the Lord will be rewarded to others who have helped me oftentimes by sprinkling grass for the rough stones, and making it easier where it would have been so hard, but for the love and prayers of God's dear children. God is preparing His church for the most glorious spectacle the universe has ever beheld, in that crowning day when the whole of creation will be summoned to gaze upon the face of the bride, the Lamb's wife, and as they gaze they will see not only the face of the Bride in all the beauty of her myriad-fold individuality, but as the unity and light of all the phases of the Lamb Himself reflected in them all, and, while it will be a picture of glorified humanity, it will be still more a picture of the Son of Man.

A dear friend has given me this beautiful illustration suggested by a single painting. Here is a woman's face. It is loveliness itself, as its features are traced upon the canvas in the soft, vivid light of Italian art. There is the perfect form, the warm color, the modest yet noble brow, the rich tresses of hair, the expression of loveliness, the repose and strength of character, all seeming to speak with the light of life itself. Such is the picture as you see it at a distance, but when you come a little closer a strange

transformation takes place. Making up that
one face you see a hundred other faces and
objects, and you find that it is a composite
painting´ made up of many minutiæ, so
shaded and compounded that at a distance
the combined effect was that of a single face,
but at closer inspection it is a cluster of many
objects. There, forming the rich color of the
lips, are exquisitely shaded flowers, the hair
is formed of trailing vines and grasses, little
faces of beautiful children fit into the countenance, rich clusters of fruit the eye, and all
blended together in infinite diversity and yet
perfect unison.

Such will be the face that this universe
will yet behold. Jesus, shining in all, all in
all. Your face will be there, in perfect identity, and yet blended in the soft light of His
countenance, and reflecting the radiance of
His smile. So let us abide in Him and grow
up together into Him, until we shall see the
fullness of the stature of Christ Jesus.

CHAPTER X.

ÒUR HORN OF SALVATION.

"Blessed be the Lord God of Israel; for He hath visited and redeemed His people, and hath raised up a horn of salvation for us in the house of His servant David; as He spake by the mouth of His holy prophet, which have been since the world began; that we should be saved from our enemies, and from the hand of all that hate us; to perform the mercy promised to our fathers, and to remember His holy covenant; the oath which He sware to our Father Abraham, that He would grant unto us, that we being delivered out of the hand of our enemies might serve Him without fear, in holiness and righteousness before Him all the days of our life." Luke i: 68–75.

ZACHARIAS, the father of John the Baptist and the author of this song, was practically the last of the priesthood. Because of his priestly office he was chosen to be the father of John the Baptist, and thus, both directly and through his son, the witness of the coming dispensation and the Messiah. God so ordered it that Judaism bore witness to Christ, although Judaism was afterwards to reject Christ notwithstanding its own testimony. True to the spirit of Judaism, when the message came to Zacharias about the birth of his son, his unbelief refused to accept it, and God visited him with dumbness and silence until the birth of John. The silence of Zacharias was significant of the silence that was to fall on Judaism as she gave place to the testimony of Christ and sank back into silence at His feet, while all heaven proclaimed, "This is my beloved Son; hear ye Him."

How different the spirit of Mary, when the message came to her requiring even greater faith! More truly she represented the spirit of Christianity. She implicitly believed it, and her answer was, "Behold the handmaid of the Lord. Be it unto me according to thy word." But at length Zacharias' lips were opened at the circumcision of his son, and with this last song his voice died away with the voice of Judaism into eternal silence. There is a beautiful bird which has but one song, and that its own death dirge. After silently sailing the waters for its whole life long, the beautiful swan at last, on the bosom of some peaceful lake, perhaps as the shadows of evening are falling and darkness is passing over its simple brain, opens its mouth, and pours out the strangest, saddest song that ever fell upon the ear, and then its beautiful, graceful neck relaxes, and it sinks upon the waves in the silence of death. It has breathed its life out in its one last song. So Zacharias passes out of view with his own song, but it was a song worthy to be lost in, for it is the key-note of redemption, and yet shall re-echo in the song of Moses and the Lamb. There are three strains in it; like all great songs, extremely simple, but swelling out into infinite echoes of glory and blessing.

I. "HE HATH VISITED HIS PEOPLE."

We love to receive the letter of our friend, but how much more the friend himself! Sweet is the message of affection, but

sweeter the visit of our loved ones! The
glory of Zacharias' song was that God was
about to visit His people. This was the cry
of Moses, "If thy presence go not with us,
carry us not up hence, for wherein shall we
differ from all the other people of the earth,
except it be that thou go with us." Not even
an angel's presence would satisfy or fill the
place, none but God Himself. This was the
burden of all Isaiah's wondrous promises.
The Lord Himself shall come to visit His
people. This is the pre-eminent glory of redemption. God Himself has undertaken it.
The Eternal One has come to our world in
person, and identified Himself forever with
humanity.

1. It tells the story of the incarnation.
"The Word was made flesh, and dwelt
among us, and we beheld His glory, the
glory as of the only begotten of the Father,
full of grace and truth." He has come into
our house of clay, and He has come to stay,
and to the latest ages of eternity, as generation after generation shall visit the metrop-

olis of the universe, and lift up their eyes to look upon God, they shall see the face of a man, a form like our own, God in the likeness of humanity. He has come so near to us that He has come into our own nature. "Forasmuch then as the children are partakers of flesh and blood, He also Himself likewise took part of the same; that through death He might destroy him that hath the power of death. For verily He took not on Him the nature of angels; but He took on Him the seed of Abraham. Wherefore it behooved Him in all things to be made like unto His brethren, that He might be a faithful and merciful high priest in things pertaining to God."

When Vanderkemp went to South Africa as a missionary, he proved his sympathy with the people, not only by living among them, but by marrying a Hottentot girl. He came down into their very life, and united his being with their degraded race to let them know that he was part of them. So Christ has wedded Himself forever to humanity, and never can be separated from us any more then we can separate ourselves from our own bodies. When the first missionaries went to St. Thomas, they could not get near the suffering and degraded slaves until they took part in their bondage, and asked the masters to make them slaves also. Then they were received with perfect confidence, and were able to bring multitudes of the poor savages to Christ. They trusted them when they saw that they had become identified with their own very life and lot. "Blessed be the Lord God of Israel; for He hath visited His people."

2. But He comes closer. These missionaries could work by the side of the slave; but they could not come into their hearts. I can sit down and talk with you in your home; but I cannot walk into your brain and into your spirit, and put my being into yours, so that you shall have my thoughts and feelings and life. In some measure love can impart almost its own soul to the beloved one, and yet only in a faint measure com-

pared with the great and divine example
which Christ has forever set us; for He hath
not only visited our race, but He hath visited our hearts, and made our very bodies
His temple and home. "With this man will
I dwell" saith the High and Holy One that
inhabiteth eternity, "Even with him that is
humble and of a contrite spirit, and who
trembleth at my word." "I will dwell in
them, and walk in them, and they shall be
my people and I will be their God."

Has He visited you, beloved? Has He come
into this brain and possessed all its thoughts,
and given to you His light and wisdom, His
understanding and mind? Has He come into this will and taken the key of the chamber from which all the acts and purposes of
your lives are directed? Has He been ad-
mitted to the boudoir chamber of your confidences, where only your dearest ones ever
come, and does He control all your heart's
affections, and supremely hold them for Himself, so that you have no life apart from Him?
Has He found His way without restraint

into every inmost apartment, until you find
they are being enlarged by His ministry, and
filled in every capacity with His love and life,
as He thinks in you, trusts in you, wills in
you, loves in you, rejoices in you, speaks in
you, prays in you, praises in you, and pours
out through your whole being the fullness of
His life; not a transient visitor, but a perpet-
ual Guest. Oh! how much He will do for the
heart that thus receives Him!

Happy for the loving woman of Shunem the
day that Elisha passed her door, that she received him in the name of the Lord, and
made him welcome to her home and her
heart. Little did she dream that it was going to bring her in the coming years deliverance from her sorrows and her trials, the
child of her affection, and that child a second
time restored from death itself. What care
He will take of the house that He owns and
lives in! How He will love to heal and
strengthen and beautify and glorify the temple of His indwelling, and what infinite rest
it is to live with Christ in His own house,

and have Him bear all the burdens and responsibilities, while you dwell a happy guest
in the house that you once called your own.

3. And then He is coming in a little while
on a still more glorious visit, with sound of
trumpet and mighty processions of angels
and ransomed men, while earth and heaven
shall signal His glorious advent by signs and
wonders such as the universe has never beheld. It is said that the great Ivan of Russia
loved to go in disguise among his people,
calling often late at night at some humble
cabin in the character of a poor wayfarer,
and watching to see how they received him.
If a welcome was given, as it often was, by
some poor and suffering family, who shared
with him their last crust, and gave him shelter in their poorly-heated dwelling, it was
very likely to happen that a few days later
the royal chariot would drive up to that door,
with the outriders and footmen, and all the
splendid pageant of royalty, while the emperor himself stepped from his chariot, and
entering the humble door, called for the

kind and loving person that had received him in his obscurity, and asking perhaps the name of the youngest child, would say, "I have adopted this child as the child of the emperor. Here is a purse of money for its immediate use. I shall educate it, and always be your friend and reward and honor you, because you received your emperor when you knew not but that he was a person like yourselves."

So, beloved, the King of Kings is passing by these days of time, a lowly man, and a wayfarer He asks a sacrifice of you. He asks a welcome from you. He asks the key of your heart's inmost chamber. Will you trust Him? The day is coming when it will be much to have one glance from His glorious face, to have Him recognize you among the myriads of the resurrection and say, "Come my little child, and sit with me on my throne, and share my kingdom; for on earth you received me, and even so do I now welcome you." Yes, He is coming again to visit our earth, and to leave it no more.

"Behold, the tabernacle of God is with men," will be the announcement of that glad day, "and He will dwell with them, and God Himself shall be with them, and they shall see His face, and His name shall be written in their foreheads, and there shall be no night there." And even when the glad Millennial age is ended, it will expand into a gladder and better time, and the new heavens shall be added to the new earth, and redeemed humanity shall colonize over all this great universe, and we may have stars for kingdoms, and worlds for our inheritance. Then shall we sing as we cannot now, "Blessed be the Lord God of Israel, for He hath visited His people."

II. "HE HATH REDEEMED HIS PEOPLE."

This is much more. That Moravian missionary could stoop to the lowly condition of the heathen of St. Thomas; but he could not set them free. He could die with them in their chains; but he could not break the fetters. But Jesus not only visited His people, but He hath redeemed them. He hath given His own freedom for ours, and the ransom suffices, and the great manifesto has gone forth. "The Spirit of the Lord God is upon me, for He hath sent me to preach deliverance to the captives, to set at liberty them that are oppressed." This word redeemed is the characteristic term of the gospel. It speaks of the crimson tint of sin and the deeper crimson of Calvary's blood. It tells of a heaven that has cost something, a salvation that is established on the eternal principles of justice and righteousness, that has met every claim of law and right, and placed the ransomed soul in as good a position as if he had never sinned.

All human hearts have an instinct that such a redemption was demanded. The rudest savage is conscious that some propitiation must be made for sin, and that evil cannot be lightly passed over even by clemency, without some satisfaction. When the proud and haughty Tarquin sat upon the bench to judge his own son, with the Roman instincts of justice he could not acquit him. When the mother pleaded for her boy with bitter tears, and brothers and sisters claimed his life, and the citizens who loved him interceded, the father could only answer, "The father loves him as much as you, but the judge must punish him," and to the lictors he was delivered without mercy, to be beaten and slain, because law and justice could know no mercy.

Very beautifully have the Hindu legends embodied this truth, and at the same time foreshadowed the mystery of the gospel through which love has triumphed over justice, and yet has left justice uncompromised and vindicated. In the ancient Hindu legends there is a story of a poor sinner pursued by the spirit of retribution in the form of a demon. Flying from its pursuer, and about to be overtaken, the sinful spirit cried to Vishnu, the goddess of Mercy, for help, and she immediately changed the fugitive into a dove. With a glad cry of gratitude the dove swept up into the air, striking her

wings upon the firmament and bore away
above her pursuer, thanking her kind deliverer. But a moment later the demon had
been changed into a hawk, and lo, she
found herself pursued by a stronger wing
and a swifter flight than her own, and she
was about to be struck down by the cruel
talons of the hawk, when suddenly she lifted
up her prayer again to Vishnu, and the goddess opened her bosom as an asylum for the
fluttering dove, and folded her wings about
her as she lay there secure from her enemy.
Then the hawk approached the goddess and
demanded his prey. "She is mine," he said,
"by every right of justice. You, Vishnu,
have declared and know, sin must be pun-
ished, and that I am entitled to my victim,
and I demand her life or its equivalent."
Vishnu answered, "I recognize your claim.
Her life you cannot have, but you may have
as much of mine as will be its equivalent."
And with that she opened her bosom to the
devourer, and bade him thrust his fierce
beak and talons into her quivering flesh un-

till he had torn from her breast as much as he would have consumed if he had devoured the little dove. Satisfied, he withdrew, and the trembling dove looked upon the bleeding breast, and knew what its life had cost its deliverer: and as it floated away a little later, with the stain of blood upon its wings, it never could forget what its redemption had meant. Beloved, you and I were that dove. Justice pursued us with every claim of right. Even God could not forego its claim, but must execute it or cease to be God; but the blessed Redeemer opened His bosom, gave His life and blood to meet the claim, bore the judgment we deserved, and now sprinkled with this precious blood, we sing, "Unto Him that loved us, and washed us from our sins in His own blood, be dominion and glory, now and forever." "Worthy is the Lamb that was slain to receive honor and power and riches and glory and blessing." "Thou hast redeemed us with thy blood, and hast made us unto God kings and priests."

"Blessed be the Lord God of Israel, for He hath visited and redeemed His people."

III. HE HATH RAISED UP AN HORN OF SALVATION FOR US.

Salvation is the fruition of redemption. Redemption purchases it, salvation realizes it and brings it into our actual experience. It is not the salvation Zacharias speaks so much of as the "horn of salvation." This bold figure, perhaps, originated in primitive times, when mighty hunters, like Nimrod, returning from the chase, loved to grace their tents with the splendid horns of the animals they had slain, the antlers of the deer, the tusks of the elephant, and the horn, perhaps, of the mighty rhinoceros. And so the word "horn" came to be the figure of beauty, power and dominion. It has passed into the imagery of inspired prophecy and song, so that we find the earthly powers described by Daniel and John as horns upon the head of the beast.

And so we find the Psalmist speaking of

God as his Horn of Salvation and his High Tower. In speaking, therefore, of Christ as a horn of salvation, Zacharias. meant to emphasize the glory and beauty of the Saviour, His supreme and universal dominion, and His infinite and divine power. It is Coronation, singing, "Bring forth the royal diadem, and crown Him Lord of all." The verse that follows explains this thought more perfectly than any words of ours can do. This glorious salvation does five things for us.

1. It delivers us from all our enemies. Christ has come to overcome everything that is against us. Never does He want us to be crushed or defeated. Always He causeth us to triumph, if we will but trust and allow Him. How beautifully does the prophet Zachariah illustrate the words of his New Testament namesake, as in his first chapter he gives us his vision of the four horns, horns that were lifted up against Judah and Jerusalem, representing the evils that are opposed to us from all sides, so that

whichever direction we look, north, south, east or west, we sometimes can see nothing but enemies. But lo! he sees following the four horns four carpenters, and as he asks the meaning of this vision he is told that these were come to fray the horns, that is, to soften them, ·to peel them down, to take their sharpness from them, to render them harmless.

How wondrously does God do this for His people! How He takes the point out of the devil's sting and the enemies' sword-thrust, and quenches all the fiery darts of the wicked one with the shield of faith, so that things that seemed sufficient to destroy us pass harmlessly away, and we wonder in great amazement at the providential goodness of our wonderful God. Each of us has often had enough perils to wreck our life and work many a time, but as we look behind we cannot even trace a shadow of the clouds that once covered all our sky, and everything that seemed against us has become a voice in the chorus, "We know that all things work together for good to them that love God."

2. After being delivered from our enemies "that we might serve Him without fear." Our fears are sometimes worse than our enemies. Who of us is there that has not spent hours and days fighting clouds that never came to rain or lightning. They seemed intensely real, and they hurt as much as if they were real. Christ comes to deliver us from all our fears. He tells us that the king of fear is the devil, and that fear from him must always be recognized. As long as we abide in Christ, it is a voice from Satan. If it is a voice from Satan it is always a lie, therefore it is not to be allowed to come into the soul. Indeed, we may turn it into a benediction, and say to Satan as he holds up the shadow, "Thank you very much, for now I know that the opposite is coming—a blessing as glorious as the shadow has been dark." This is the way to get the victory over your fears. Refuse them and extract good out of them, even as the woman of Canaan did

from her Saviour's refusal, and from the
dark and discouraging prospect that for a
time seemed to overshadow all her case.
God cannot use you fully in His service if
you are loaded down with a pack of worries.
You must be rested workers. You must
come to Him for rest and then take His
yoke upon you.

3. All our sins. "In holiness and righteousness before Him." You will observe
that it is not righteousness and holiness, but
holiness first. We begin often the wrong
way, and try to get our lives right before our
hearts are pure. Like Elisha, let us go up
to the spring yonder, and put salt there, and
not in the channels of the river below.
Cleanse the fountain and the waters will always be pure. Get the holiness of Christ in
your heart, and your life will be regulated
with the full tides of life and love. Divine
life regulates itself, and the more it overflows
the more it purifies.

4. "All our days." We used to think that
holiness and victory were for our last days,

and that if we got too near to God we were being prepared to die, and might soon go; indeed, that it was not very safe to be to devout. But thank God, we have found that holiness is to live by, and that we need it for earth's duties and trials much more even than for heavenly enjoyments. Christ sanctifies us to serve Him without fear, in holiness and righteousness before Him all the days of our life. We can spring into the very fullness of His grace from the very morning of our conversion. We can go from Egypt to Canaan in less than three months; and need not spend forty years wandering in the wilderness of Sin. "Oh, if I only had known of this twenty-five years ago, how sweetly I could have lived," said the dying Payson as he stood in the last moments of his life looking into heaven, and realizing the full salvation that he might have known all his days. Beloved, shall we take him for all the days, and go forth singing,

"I'm so glad that I've to learned to trust Him,
Precious Jesus, Saviour, Friend;

And I know that thou art with me,
  Wilt be with me to the end."

There are two closing thoughts suggested
by this figure, on which we shall dwell for
a moment. In the blessing of Joseph in Deu-
teronomy xxxiii: it is said that his horns
shall be like the horns of the unicorn. The
unicorn has only one horn, and the idea
suggested by the strong figure is that they
alone are strong who have no strength but
God. The glory of my strength is to have
God alone. God is never the fullness of
power to us until He alone is our power, until we can say, "Whom have I in heaven
but thee, and there is none upon the earth
that I desire apart from thee."

The other reference is in connection with
the sublime vision of the Lamb in the fifth
chapter of Revelation, where we behold
Him standing in the midst of the throne
having seven horns and seven eyes, representing the seven-fold power and authority
with which He is invested, and the seven-
fold wisdom of the Holy Ghost which He
administers.

It is as the Lamb that He has the seven horns. It is because He suffered and redeemed us that God has invested Him, not only with His own eternal deity and power, but with all the resources of the Father's own fullness, so that He could say as He ascended from earth to heaven, "All power is given unto me, in heaven and in earth." And yet that power is in the hands of one whom John describes as a "Little Lamb." Oh! the ineffable gentleness and nearness combined with majesty and power expressed by this figure. With a hand as soft as a child's, a touch as gentle as a mother's, and yet a sceptre as mighty as omnipotence, He sits ·on yonder throne, so near and yet so great, so tender and yet so mighty, the blended gentleness and almightiness of the Lamb that is in the midst of the throne.

He is our horn of salvation. He hath visited us and redeemed us, and He must reign until all our enemies shall be made His footstool. Let us join in the chorus that swells in this chapter in billows and billows of

praise, surging and surging out to the con-
fines of the universe until "every creature
which is in heaven, and on the earth, and
under the earth, and such as are in the sea,
and all that are in them, are heard saying,
blessing and honor, and glory and power be
unto Him that sitteth upon the throne, and
unto the Lamb forever and ever."

CHAPTER XI.

THE KEY OF DAVID.

"These things saith He that is holy, He that is true, He that hath the key of David, He that openeth and no man shutteth, and shutteth and no man openeth." Rev. iii: 7.

THE seven Epistles to the Churches in Revelation contain the last message of Christ to the church of to-day. It would seem very natural to suppose that the seven churches which He chose to receive these final messages were in some respect representative of the whole Catholic church to the end of time. They are singularly descriptive of the epochs that have passed over the church since the days of John. The first, the church in Ephesus perfectly represents the church of the days of John, strong in works, but beginning to decline in love. The next, Smyrna, is true to the life of the next age of Christianity, the age of persecution. The third, the church in Pergamos, has some strong resemblance to the worldly church of the days of Constantine and succeeding emperors. The church in Thyatira is almost a perfect type of the apostasy which followed through the rise of the Papacy, with that woman Jezebel on the throne and the depths of Satan beneath her seat of ecclesiastical pride and wickedness. Then comes the church in Sardis. "Thou hast a name that thou livest and art dead." This is a sure and perfect type of the middle ages, and the absolute death of spiritual life, with the exception of a few names, even in Sardis, "Who had not defiled their garments."

Then there is a sudden burst of light— the church of Philadelphia. This message is all promise, encouragement and love. It is the dawn of Reformation. It is the gathering out of the little flock before the end. They have kept His word, they have not denied His name; they shall be kept through the hour of temptation and tribulation. They shall be established as pillars in the temple of God. They shall be enrolled in the New Jerusalem. They shall be received into the intimacy of Jesus. They shall have an open door which none can shut. There is one more picture, the church of the Laodiceans, strong, proud, wealthy, self-sufficient, lukewarm, and about to be rejected. This is the second apostasy. It is apostate Protestantism. It is the worldly church, which already in our day is beginning to show signs of this final portrait; and with it comes the Master's hand upon the door, and the solemn warning, "I stand at the door and knock." The end is just about to come. But in the previous picture the end is also about to come, and the solemn message even there is; "Behold, I come quickly. Hold fast that which thou hast, that no man take thy garment," so that these two pictures of Philadelphia and Laodicea both belong to the end. The one is the picture of the little flock of simple faithful ones; the other is the picture of the great worldly church contemporary with Philadelphia, and about to be rejected by the Lord at His coming.

It is of this sixth picture of the little Philadelphian church that we wish to speak this morning, or rather of the Master in the attitude in which He addresses it, and the precious names He Himself assumes as He addresses to them His cheering message. There are three great and blessed names.

I. HE THAT IS HOLY.

1. He is holy, therefore He expects us to be holy; for His message is, "Be ye holy, for I am holy." He is our example, our standard, and we can never rest behind His footsteps.

2. He is holy, therefore He enables us to be holy. His holiness is the source of ours, as well as the sanction and the ground of obligation; for He gives us His own holiness. He enters our heart and becomes our life, and lives in us His own pure,

heavenly life. Therefore the apostle has said, "For both He that sanctifieth, and they that are sanctified are all of one, for which cause He is not ashamed to call them brethren." Therefore He Himself said in His own parting prayer, for their sakes I sanctify myself, that they also may be truly sanctified."

This did not mean that Christ required to be made holy, as if He were unholy, but He devoted Himself in the sense of entire consecration to this one thing, the sanctification of His people. He set Himself apart for our sakes that we might be truly sanctified, as it reads in the margin; and as we receive Him to dwell within us we receive the sanctification. We receive the Holy One and He becomes our holiness, and is "made unto us of God sanctification and redemption." This is the secret of our holiness, to receive Him that is holy, to abide in Him that is holy, and to let Him live in us His own heavenly life.

II. HE THAT IS TRUE.

This is the picture of the Faithful Promiser. It means His words are true. "Hath He said, and shall He not do it? Hath He spoken, and shall He not make it good." How many precious words of promise has He spoken. How many things has He spoken to us. How many has He to speak to us to-day. Earth and heaven shall pass away, but one jot or one tittle of His promises shall in no wise pass away, until all be fulfilled. Every one of them has come to us with the mighty preface, "Thus saith He that is true." Let us rest in them, let us wait for them, for though they tarry, they shall surely come, and they shall not tarry too long. He Himself has endorsed them, and is their personal Guarantee.

On an old mosque in Syria there is a strange and beautiful illustration of God's eternal and-unchanging word. It was a Christian church and it had on its front, worked in the stone, the words of God, "Thy kingdom is an everlasting kingdom,

and thy truth endureth to all generations."
When the Moslems conquered Palestine,
they captured the old church, and plastered
over the front, and in blazing and re-
splendant letters of gold they wrote another
inscription in honor of the false prophet.
But as the centuries have gone by the
plaster has fallen off. The transient record
of human sin and pride has perished, and
the deeply written record of God's Word
stands out bold and clear, as a solemn in-
timation that all men's works and words
shall pass away, but the word of our God
shall stand forever.

But it means much more than this. Back
of all is His own true heart. He Himself is
true, our faithful unchangable Friend, and
the Guarantee of the certainty and stability
of everything that we value and hold in
Him. God is much more to the Christian's
faith than even His word. Abraham believed God, and therefore He believed His
word. It is because we can trust Him that
we can trust His promises. How we value

a true heart. How we rest in a faithful friend. How we love to lean on one that we know is loyal to the core. Christ is absolutely true. He loved us from the beginning. He will love us to the end. It is because He chose us knowing all, anticipating all, prepared for the worst that His love is everlasting. He is so true that He will keep us true. Think of some of the assurances of His faithfulness. He hath said, "I will never leave nor forsake thee." God is faithful, by whom ye were called into the fellowship of His Son, Jesus Christ.

"He will also confirm you to the end, that ye may be blameless in the day of Jesus Christ. God is faithful, who will not suffer you to be tempted above that which ye are able; but will, with the temptation, make also a way of escape; that ye may be able to bear it." "Wherefore, let them that suffer according to the will of God, commit the keeping of their souls to Him in well doing, as unto a faithful Creator." "The very God of peace sanctify you wholly, and

I pray God your whole spirit and soul and body be preserved blameless unto the coming of our Lord Jesus Christ." "Faithful is He that calleth you, who also will do it " So that we have the faithfulness of God vouched for our sanctification, for our preservation, for our deliverance, for our temptation, for our comfort and support in trial and suffering, for all we can trust Him up to the coming of our Lord Jesus Christ; and we can trust Him with all our heart, with all our weight, casting all our care upon Him, for He careth for us, trusting in the Lord Jehovah forever, for He is the Rock of Ages.

But still further, " He that is true " is the Guarantee of our true-heartedness and stability. He will keep us true. We can take Him for our steadfastness. Not only is God at the heaven-side to anchor the cable yonder; but He is also at the heart-side, through the Holy Ghost, to fasten it here, so that it will not slip as it holds us. And so this precious epistle is full of promises of keeping. While on the one side it bids us hold

fast that which we have, that no man take
our crown, on the other it promises, "I
will keep you from the hour of temptation
which cometh upon all the world to try all
that they dwell upon the whole earth," and
still more strongly, "I will make you a
pillar in the temple of my God, and ye shall
go no more out." Thank God we can take
Him for our courage, for our steadfastness,
for "He is able to keep us from falling,
and to present us faultless before the presence of His glory with exceeding joy."
Blessed is He that is holy, He that is true.

III. HE THAT HATH THE KEY OF DAVID.

This, of course, is a description of Christ
as a King, as the real successor to David,
King of Israel, the Sovereign, Lord of Nature, Providence, the Church, and the Millennial world, the One that controls all destinies, and possesses all power and dominion
in heaven and in earth. But more particularly, as the holder of the Key of David,
" He openeth, and no man shutteth; and He
shutteth, and no man openeth."

1. How many things He opens, and opens for ever to His people! He opens the gates of life; for "I am the door, by me if any man enter in he shall be saved, and shall go in and out, and find pastures." He opens the gate of heaven; for into that city shall enter they only that are written in the Lamb's book of life, and over the gate are written the words, "Blessed are they that wash their robes, that they may have right to the tree of life, and may enter through the gates into the city." He opens our heart for His incoming. He opened Lydia's heart. He won our stubborn will, and taught us to trust and love Him, and yield ourselves to Him, and He alone can rule us and subdue us with His sceptre of perfect love.

He opens our eyes to understand His will, and He opens His word to our understanding, so that we may behold wondrous things out of His law, and possess all the treasures of His glorious truth. He opens for us the gates of difficulty, and breaks in pieces the gates of brass, and cuts in sunder the bars of iron, and enables us to go forward through what seem impassible barriers in His work and will. He holds the key of knowledge, and opens to us every problem that perplexes, and every question that baffles, and will be our wisdom and guide in every trying hour.

He opens our way of service, our doors of usefulness, and prepares us for them, for our work, and our field, and He says to us, "Behold, I have set before thee an open door, and no man can shut it." He prepared Paul's work and gave it to him, and He will give you yours if you are ready to do it, and none can hinder, for when He gives it, everything must go away. He holds the key of human hearts, and can open them to your message. He can convict the conscience, influence the will, persuade the heart, draw the sinner to His feet, and constrain the reluctant to be willing in the day of His power. He holds the key to every safe and pocket-book, and He can say to you, "I will give thee the treasures of darkness, and the hidden riches of secret places," and He will provide the means that you need for every undertaking on which He sends you.

He holds the key of providence, and can control all events and circumstances in your external life, to co-operate with you, or become tributary to you in your service for Him. He that opened the prison gates for Peter, and rent the bars of the Philippian jail is still the same. He who gave Esther and Daniel favor in the courts of Persia and Babylon, and made Joseph to be beloved of all he met in the land of Egypt, and gave Paul the friendship of the captain of the guard and made Cyrus in the flush of his pride send forth the captives of Israel to their land, He can still open every door and control every heart. "The king's heart is in the hand of the Lord, and He turneth it whithersoever He will, as the rivers of waters," and He will open for you the pathway of His will, the way in which He would have you go. "I will lead the blind," He says, "by a way that they know not. I will lead them

in paths that they have not known. I will
make the darkness light before them, and
the crooked things straight. These things
will I do unto you and not forsake them.
I have raised them up in righteousness, and
I will direct all His ways, I will work, and
who will let it." His people's path may
lead through Red Seas, and Jordans of
swollen tides, and Jerichos of formidable
and definite power, and Euroclydian's wild
tempestuous fire; but He who has already
burst through the gates of death and hell
will fulfill all His counsel, and accomplish
all His perfect will.

> "When He makes bare His arm,
> Who shall His power withstand,
> When He His people's cause maintains,
> Who, who shall stay His hand."

Beloved, will you use your key more faithfully, more trustfully, more constantly?
Will you prove more fully than ever that
you have One with you "who openeth and
no man shutteth?"

2. How many things He shuts! He has

shut for us the gates of hell, blessed be His name forever. "And there is no condemnation now to them that are in Christ Jesus; and they shall not come into judgment, but have passed out of death into life." He holds the keys of death, and its darts cannot touch His children until He permits them. He holds back the gates of temptation. Satan cannot touch one of His children even with a tormenting thought till the Master permits. There is an "if need be" in our manifold temptations. We are led out of the Spirit into the wilderness to be tempted of the devil. Between every dragon wing, and every hellish dart and us is the presence of the Holy Ghost, and the bosom of Jesus, and the shield of faith, and "He that was begotten of God keepeth us and that wicked one touch us not." And therefore He says in this verse, "Because thou hast kept the word of my patience, I will keep thee from the hour of temptation that cometh upon all the world." This probably means the last and terrible tribulation from which the saints of

God shall be taken out and preserved; but it also means many another hour of temptation from which His people are free. One of the terrible calamities of the wicked is that they are tempted above that which they are able to bear; but one of the most blessed promises to the saints is that he shall not be so tempted, but that he shall be guarded, and when the pressure would be too strong it shall be held back.

He also keeps back the floods of sorrow and calamity. In the seventh chapter of Revelation we behold an angel standing in the sky and holding back the winds, lest they should blow upon the earth before the saints of God were sealed. And so God shuts the doors of the natural world, the flood-gates of the tides of all evil, and says, " Thus far shalt thou come and no further," and here shall the waves be stopped. Fear not, He will deliver you in trial. The floods may have lifted up their voice and made a mighty noise. But the Lord that is on high is mightier than the noise of many waters, and the great sea billows. The Lord sitteth King above the floods; yea, the Lord sitteth King forever. There is another door that He shuts, and that is the door of the inner chamber, where He hides us with Himself, where He takes us into His fellowship, where He gives us His eternal covenant, and seals and secures to us that "which we have committed unto Him against that day."

In this closing verse He says, "I will make Him a pillar in the temple of my God, and the name of the city of my God, which is New Jerusalem, which cometh down from heaven out of God, and I will write upon Him my new name." When God put Noah in the ark He shut him in. When He takes us into His bosom He shuts us in. When He gives us His promises He guarantees them, and seals them, and keeps them for us.

The ideas underlying these beautiful figures are stability, security and intimacy. He will keep us. He will make us a part of Himself, which is the meaning of the

name of God. He will make us a part and
parcel of the New Jerusalem, giving us a
place in His millennial glory, and writing
the very name of that city upon us as if we
inseparably belonged to it. And He will
give us the pledge of His own personal and
pure intimacy, writing upon us His own
new name. This refers back to the white
stone and the name written upon it, which
no man could read except he to whom it
was given. This is the token of the secret
love, the special covenant, the confidential
friendship, the inmost, uttermost love of
Jesus.

Now unto Him that is holy, that is true,
that hath the key of David, "that openeth
and no man shutteth, that shutteth and no
man openeth, be glory forever." And He
answers back to us, "Behold, I have set
before thee an open door, and no man can
shut it." It opens up to the glory of His
coming, and with the crown shining in the
light of vision just before, as He cries,
"Behold, I come quickly; hold fast that

which thou hast, that no man take thy crown." And we take Him to hold us, and to hold for us our crown, and then to let us lay it at His blessed feet forever and say, "Thou who art holy, thou who art true, thou who hast given all and kept all, thou shalt have all the glory forever. Amen."

CHAPTER XII.

THE CORNER.

"Out of him shall come forth the corner, out of him the nail, out of him the battle-bow." Zechariah x: 4.

THE reference of this verse is to the tribe of Judah, out of which was to come the corner, the nail and the battle-bow. This may have referred, in the first instance, to earthly kings and defenders, but undoubtedly their ultimate typical application was to the Lord Jesus Christ, and to Him indeed the same figures are elsewhere applied so explicitly as to leave no doubt as to the scripturalness of this interpretation.

I. THE CORNER.

This metaphor is directly applied to the Lord Jesus Christ by the apostle Peter in the second chapter of his first Epsitle, fourth verse, "To whom coming, as unto a living stone, disallowed indeed of men, but chosen of God and precious, ye also as lively stones, are built up a spiritual house, an holy priesthood, to offer up spiritual sacrifices, acceptable to God by Christ Jesus. Wherefore also it is contained in the Scripture, 'Behold I lay in Zion a chief corner-stone, elect, precious; and he that believeth on Him shall not be confounded.' Unto you therefore which believe, He is precious; but unto them which be disobedient, the stone which the builders disallowed, the same is made the head of the corner."

1. The corner-stone is the foundation of the building. It rests upon it. So Christ is our foundation. There we rest our hopes for eternity and for everything. "Other foundation can no man lay than that which is laid, which is Christ Jesus."

2. The corner-stone regulates the entire building. From the corner-stone all the other locations and measurements are taken. So Christ gives direction to all our life. Everything should be shaped with reference

to Him as the centre. We can build no broader than the foundation and corner, and so our lives can never pass beyond Christ, but simply be the filling up of that which . He has already in Himself. The plumb line falls till it reaches the corner-stone, and the walls must be ever vertical to it or they will fall. Our whole Christian life must be under the absolute control of the Lord Jesus, and both in its lateral and vertical lines, as it reaches toward others and touches heaven, it must be according to His mind and will, His Spirit and holy example.

3. The corner-stone unites the building. Without it there can be only one wall, and a wall is not a building. It is in Jesus that we touch each other and become united in our Christian life and in our inmost Spirit. A common creed will never unite us; a common work will not permanently unite us; only a common life will. The true secret of catholicity in the church is to live closer to Jesus. A deep spiritual life will always sweep away the consciousness, at least, of

sectarian barriers. Would we love each other and be closely united, let us be filled with His love, and, pressing hard to His bosom, we shall touch each other in the sweetest fellowship of Christian life.

4. The corner-stone bears the record of the building. The name is upon the stone, and so we should bear the name of Jesus, and no name be seen but His. The date is there, and, although the stone was laid long before the finishing of the building, yet the edifice always bears the date of the stone. So the true date of our salvation is Calvary and the resurrection. It was then that we died with Him, it was then that we rose with Him, it was then that our salvation, our healing, our redemption was finished, and we simply now receive the completed work of Christ. And so the story of the building is written upon His hands and His feet, and upon His heart, and the eternal recompenses will be given according to the inscriptions that He holds.

5. The corner-stone is the ornamental

stone of the building. It is often made of polished granite or marble, or still more precious material, and it is the object of observation, and the ornament of the structure. So Jesus bears the glory. Unto you, therefore, which believe He is precious, or literally, is for an ornament. We are not to bear the praise or the glory, or to decorate ourselves with the insignia of human grandeur, but to be hidden upon His bosom, and to hold Him up before the world as our honor and our praise, ever crying, "Blessing, and glory, and riches, and honor, and thanksgiving, and power, and might, be unto the Lamb forever and forever.

"Not I, but Christ, be honored, praised, exalted;
   Not I, but Christ, be seen, be known, be heard.
Not I, but Christ, in every look and motion;
   Not I, but Christ, in every thought and word.
Oh, to be saved from myself, dear Lord,
   Oh, to be lost in thee;
Oh, that it might be no more I,
   But Christ that lives in me."

II. THE NAIL.

In the twenty-second chapter of Isaiah this figure is more fully referred to:

"And the key of the house of David will I lay upon His shoulder; so He shall open and none shall shut, and he shall shut and none shall open. And I will fasten him as a nail in a sure place, and he shall be for a glorious throne for his father's house. And they shall hang upon Him all the glory of his father's house, the offspring and the issue, all vessels of small quantity, from the vessels of cups even to all the vessels of flagons."

In the third chapter of Revelation this passage is quoted by the Lord Jesus Himself with respect to Himself:

" These things saith He that is holy, He that hath the key of David, He that openeth and no man shutteth, and shutteth and no man openeth."

The passage here refers directly to Christ, and it is in this passage that He is called the "Nail fastened in the sure place," on which is to be hung all the glory of the Father's house. There are two special uses of a nail. The first is to secure and fasten, and so

Christ is the security of our hopes and lives. He keeps us by His intercession, by His life, by our union with Himself. Secondly, a nail is to hang things upon, and this is the special sense in which it is here used. The Father has hung everything upon Jesus. All the glory of the Father's house is upon Him. "All things are delivered unto me of my Father," He says. "The Father loveth the Son, and hath given all things into His hands." There is no attribute of power, wisdom or love in God which Jesus does not fully possess, and has not the right to communicate to us or use for our well-being. But not only has the Father hung everything upon Him, but He can hang all our graces upon Him. We are not to hang them upon ourselves. We do not and never shall possess anything of ourselves. It is not that we are to add our virtues to our own person, but we are to take Christ to be in our hearts "as a nail fastened in a sure place," and then upon Him we may hang the faith, the love, the peace, the gentleness, the patience, and all the graces of spirit, until our heart becomes a wardrobe with a thousand dresses ready for use as we need them in each new situation and act of life.

The figure represents the nail as bearing upon it, not only all the glory of the Father's house, but the offspring and the issue, and all vessels, both the small vessels and vessels of flagons. The offspring and issue have reference, perhaps, to our being born ourselves of Him as His very offspring and issue, and fastened to Him by ties of blood and life; or it may refer to our offspring and issue, our spiritual fruit, all of which we must receive through Him, for our power is not our own, but is hung upon Christ, and all our work must be handed over to Him and kept by Him as the nail on which we leave every precious thing. The vessels and flagons hung upon this nail have reference to the various needs of life, all of which are supplied from Him. On this blessed nail are hanging cups of every size, which we can fill, and from which we can drink whenever we are thirsty, and there is no want so small but we can find it met in His name, and life, and love. The flagons, or vessels of wine, refer to the deeper joys, blessings of our communion with Him. As there is no cup too small for Him to fill, so there is no need too deep, no joy too divine, for Him to satisfy.

The sure place in which this nail is fastened has reference to the certainty and security of the blessing which we have in Christ. All else is liable to fail, but that which we hang upon Him will stand forever. The confidences we repose in others and ourselves are fragile; but this only can never be removed. This hope is an anchor of the soul, both sure and steadfast.

First, this nail has been fastened into the cross of Calvary, where our salvation was completed.

Secondly, this nail has been fastened into the throne in the ascension and resurrection of Christ, guaranteeing our complete salvation, and

Thirdly, it may be fastened in our hearts as the very essence and substance of our inmost life, a life so certain, a keeping so infinite and divine, that we can say, "I know whom I have believed, and am persuaded that He is able to keep that which I have committed unto Him against that day."

There are two ways of fastening a nail. One is to drive a cut nail into the wood, and just leave it. The other is to take a wrought nail, made of malleable iron, and drive it through and a little beyond, and then clinch it. This kind of work never draws, and this is the sort of nail that Christ is, when truly taken in the committal of faith.

Christ has clinched the nail on His side. "I give unto them eternal life, and they shall never perish, neither shall any pluck them out of my hand." This is the nail driven; but listen, "My Father which gave them to me is greater than all; and none is able to pluck them out of my Father's hand." That is the nail clinched.

III. THE BATTLE-BOW.

The first thing suggested by the bow is that Christ is the spring of our lives. If you want a spirit that sweeps the heavens, and reaches out into the infinite possibilities of God's boundlessness, take Christ to dwell in your heart.

Next, the figure suggests defence. Christ is our defence against the enemy; but we have to use Him as you would use a bow. A bow lying on the ground is of no use. A bow unstrung is of no use; but you must take it and draw the string, and pull the bow, and shoot the arrow, and your enemies shall fall with every shaft.

Again, the bow suggests an arrow. The bow is useless without an arrow. The arrows are God's promises and our prayers, pointed by definite desires, directed by the will of God, winged by faith and holy expectation, and then sent forth with the strong hand and the full momentum of the faith of God to reach the heavens and the

uttermost parts of our needs and our difficulties.

We have a beautiful example of these
arrows in the thirteenth chapter of second
Kings. The great prophet of Israel was
dying, and Jehoash, his grateful king, came
to visit him, and cried, as he knelt beside
him, O my father, my father, the chariot of
Israel and the horsemen thereof. Then
Elisha proceeded to give the king some
expression and evidence of his real help,
stronger than mere words. He bade Him
take a bow and arrows that were lying by
his side, and, putting his hands alongside
the king's, he commanded him to pull the
string to its utmost tension, and shoot an
arrow; and as it sped away into the fields
beyond, he cried, "The arrow of the Lord's
deliverance, and the arrow of deliverance
from Syria, for thou shalt smite the Syrians
in Aphek, till thou have consumed them."
But this was not enough. He must now
take up the arrows and prove for himself
the strength and completeness of His faith,

and so the prophet bids him smite upon the ground. He does it thrice, and then stops. The old prophet looks grave and angry. "Thou shouldst have smitten five or six times; then hadst thou smitten Syria till thou hadst consumed it; whereas thou shalt smite Syria but thrice." He had only taken half a blessing, and that was all that he should have. What a beautiful type of faith which our text expresses!

As we take the bow of faith, there is another hand that holds and guides it. Let us not fear to pull the string to its utmost tension, for this bow will never break. Christ is the battle-bow, and His hand is pulling the string with ours, and we can have all we dare to claim. Let the arrow be very definite, and then let us not stay until we have covered the whole circle of possible need and blessing, and He will be only too glad to give us all we dare to claim, and grieved only because we take so little. May the Lord help us to know "the exceeding greatness of His power to usward who

believe, according to the working of His
mighty power which He wrought in Christ,
when He raised Him from the dead and set
Him at His own right hand in the heavenly
places, far above all might, and principality,
and power, and dominion, and every name
that is named, not only in this world, but in
that which is to come!"

CHAPTER XIII.

THE REFINER.

"But who may abide the day of His coming, and who shall stand when He appeareth, for He is like a refiner's fire, and like fuller's sope? And He shall sit as a refiner and purifier of silver: and He shall purify the sons of Levi, and purge them as gold and silver, that they may offer unto the Lord an offering in righteousness." Malachi iii: 2, 3.

THIS is the last Old Testament prophetic message respecting the coming Messiah. The first verse tells of two messengers who are soon to appear: one is the forerunner, the other the Saviour, the great angel of the covenant who appeared to Abraham and Moses, and who in the Old Testament ages was the manifestation of Jehovah to His people. The special reference is to His purifying work. He is to be distinguished from all former teachers and messengers by His sin-cleansing power. He is to "sit as a refiner and purifier of silver, and to purify the sons of Levi that they may offer an offering in righteousness." Other messengers could bring reformation; but He is to bring regeneration. Others were reprovers of sin; but He brings the power that takes the sin away.

Malachi's message was echoed four centuries later by John the Baptist as he stood among the thousands who came to Him for deliverance from their sins, and he felt his helplessness to grant them what they needed, and longed for a stronger and diviner hand to cleanse and keep. "I indeed baptize you with water unto repentance," but while he said it he knew that the men who came to him to confess their sins would ere long be again immersed in sin and powerless to overcome it, and he longed intensely for one who could not only reprove and forgive, but who could renew and radically cleanse the heart from intrinsic evil. And so he added: "There cometh one after me whose shoe latchet I am not worthy to stoop down and unloose: He shall

baptize with the Holy Ghost and with fire."
This was indeed the meaning of the glorious
name given to the Saviour before He came,
"Jesus, for He shall save His people from
their sins," and this is one of the radical
distinctions between the Old Testament and
the New. The latter provides for a complete and perfect cleansing and purification
of our entire being from the power of evil,
such as the law could never bring.

Let us inquire for a little what are the
essential differences between the Old and
the New Testaments, the Law and the
Gospel in the provision they make for our
spiritual cleansing.

I.

First, Christ brings us a far higher standard, no less, indeed, than a divine example.
His command to us is, "Be ye holy as I am
holy." "Be ye therefore perfect even as
your Father which is in heaven is perfect."
He requires of us not only a lofty human
character, but complete resemblance to the

divine image. "Love one another as I have loved you." "He has chosen us that we should be conformed to the image of His Son." "Put on the new man which is renewed in holiness after the image of Him that created him." He that abideth in Him ought to walk even as He walked.

But not only does it unfold a higher standard, but it reveals a deeper, more interior life, a life that reaches even to the heart, the thoughts, the motives, the desires; which requires us to love the Lord with all our heart, and soul, and mind, and strength, to not only abstain from impurity, but from unholy thought and feeling, not only to do right, but to do right from a right motive. The word for purity in the New Testament is singleness of heart, murder is hatred, adultery is evil desire, and the righteousness of the kingdom a radical and divine renewing of the inmost being and all the principles, motives, and aims of life.

Not only so, but the righteousness of the New Testament reaches to all sides of our being and relationships, internal as well as external. The Old Testament had sacred persons, times, and things; but under the New Testament everything is sacred. One day in seven was holy to the Lord; but now every day should be a Sabbath in its true spirit. One place was His sanctuary; but now every place should be dedicated to His glory. One class of men were separated to sacred priestly functions; but now we are "all kings and priests unto God," and expected to be equally holy and near to Him. One class of duties was holier than another; but now everything we do may be done unto His glory, and pleasing in His sight.

And so the standard of New Testament holiness is higher, deeper, and broader than the Old. Therefore, we find some things even in the morality of the former which would not be accepted under the New. Zechariah, the prophet, dying under the hand of Joash, prays, "Lord, look upon it and require it." Stephen looks up from the blows of his murderers and cries, "Lord, lay not this sin to their charge."

II.

But secondly, Christ makes complete provision in His atonement for our cleansing. The offerings of the Old Testament were types of this future provision for the cleansing of the offerer; but the apostle well says in Hebrews, "they never could make the comers thereunto perfect," but Christ has come with His own blood to make full and final provision for our entire cleansing. "It is not possible that the blood of bulls and goats should take away our sins." "Then said He, Lo, I come to do thy will, O God; by the which will we are sanctified through the offering of the body of Jesus Christ once for all." "For by one offering He hath perfected forever them that are sanctified." It is therefore true that the atonement of Jesus Christ has provided for our entire cleansing from evil, and the sanctification of our entire being to God. If this be so, whatever the difficulties may be, it is our redemption right, and if it be so, it is the redemption right of all believers. It is not an exclusive or exceptional distinction which a few saintly ones may claim, but it is covered by the blood of the cross and the whosoever of the gospel, and if we are not entering into it as a personal experience, we are to that extent allowing Christ to have died for us in vain and coming short of the full inheritance. Beloved, do- you realize that it is your privilege, your purchased right, to be holy, and that for this purpose your Saviour shed His precious blood, and you are stabbing Him with a new wound if you let Him die in vain.

III.

Thirdly, Christ has not only revealed a higher holiness and purchased for us the right to it; but He has risen again to become for us the living source of that holiness through union with His own person; and He has offered to come to us in His person, and to become to each of us an indwelling life which will literally reproduce in us His own purity and enable us to live among men even as He lived. This is something which the Old Testament saints never knew. God was *with* Moses and Elijah, and the men at Babylon; but God is *in* the humblest of His saints who sincerely receive Him. This is the mystery hid from ages and generations, "Christ in you, the hope of glory." This is "the wisdom of God in a mystery, even the wisdom which none of the princes of this world knew," Christ "made unto us of God wisdom, even righteousness, sanctification and redemption." This is the great provision of the gospel, a living personal Saviour, Christ our life. This is our all sufficiency for every situation and trial, and difficulty, "I can do all things through Christ, who is my strength." This is the source of holy living, and holy usefulness, "He that abideth in me, and I in him, the same bringeth forth much fruit, for apart from me ye can do nothing." This renders our failures inexcusable. This makes our responsibility for a holy life ten-fold greater. Beloved, have we recognized that God is meeting

each of us with a full divine provision for a
life of holiness and victory, and that He
holds us responsible, not so much to do it
ourselves, as to receive from Him the grace
and power that will enable us to do it.

IV.

Fourth. The pre-eminent provision Jesus
Christ has made in the gospel for our cleansing is the gift of the Holy Ghost.   He sent
to us from heaven the third person of the
Divine Trinity to take up His abode in our
heart, to impart to us the very life of Christ,
to teach us, to lead us, train us in our
Christian life, and to carry on the whole
work of our cleansing and spiritual perfect-
ing, until the Refiner can see His image
mirrored in the silver, and we are prepared
to be jewels in the day of His coming.   It is
to this deeper, quieter, more patient working
of the Holy Ghost that the text specially refers.   It is one thing to be cleansed from sin,
and surely that ought to be true of every
Christian, but it is a differnt thing to be

refined by God's holy fire until we have been brought into all the fullness of His will, and reflect in all things His holy image. It is this thorough work of the Holy Ghost to which God is calling us in these words, where He *sits* as "a refiner and purifier of silver," calming, working and waiting until His purpose is fulfilled.

In the picture given of the Holy Bride as she sits waiting for the coming Lord, it is said in the book of Revelation that it was granted to her to be arrayed in fine linen, clean and bright, or lustrous. It is one thing to have the linen clean: it is another to have it bright and lustrous. You may take your linen from the clothes line, and there is no spot on it; but when you take it from the laundry, it is not only spotless, but lustrous, polished, shining with the gloss of skillful hands; and if it be costly embroidery, or lace adorned with all the delicate touches of the needle and the loom, arranged in beautiful order and taste. It is one thing for the gold to be cleansed from the dross:

it is another for it to be shaped in all the skill of the silversmith's art. It is one thing to have sin burned out: it is quite another to have the glory burned in.

And so we read again in Daniel, " many shall be purified, and made white and tried." The purification is the primary work of sanctification; but the making white is that which John expresses by the word *lustrous*, it is the refining, the adorning, the completing of the work in the minutiæ of detail. This is the work which the Holy Ghost is carrying on in all our hearts as fully as we will let Him. Perhaps He has delivered you from sin; but now He is endeavoring to deliver you from self. There is nothing more truly productive of miseries and failures in Christian life than the spirit of self, even in good persons.

Ask yourself this morning whence all your cares and worries come, and you will find from some thought of self, from some fear about yourself, from some consideration of your interests, rights, wrongs, grievances, or troubles. It will be a heaven of rest to you, and a source of great blessing to others, if you will wholly cancel all thoughts of yourself, and will truly say that all your acts and prayers are for others, and for your Master's cause; and the moment you begin to live this life you will enter into perfect peace, and you will find that God has taken up your cause.

Or, again, He is, perhaps, refining you from your natural life and lifting you into a spiritual life and love. Your affections are, perhaps, merely human, and they are absorbing others for your own gratification rather than for God's will and glory, and are keeping you on a lower plane. God wants them transformed and transfigured -into the heavenly love that will be abiding and eternal, the millennial life into which He is leading you already, even before the coming of your Lord. He is crucifying you to your loves and links, that they may be reformed in God, and so formed that they may be forever.

Have you ever seen a skeletonized bouquet?
Look at those leaves as they are in their
natural beauty; they are soft and green, but
fading; in a few hours they will wither
away, and their beauty will be dead. But
look at them after some skillful woman's
hands have touched them and they have
come forth from the bleaching whiter than
the driven snow, delicate, ethereal, as
flowers of paradise, every fibre of the
skeleton standing out in fine and clear relief, and yet so purified from the earthly
and fleshly covering that they are more
beautiful than before, and withall you know
are now abiding. Their beauty will never
wither. They stand in your vase or cabinet
the same through the passing years, the
substance of that which you once possessed
in a lower form. It is a cold and imperfect
figure, yet it expresses something of the
refining process through which God is putting our hearts and transforming our earthly loves into heavenly ties that will last
forever, not like those dry, skeletonized

leaves, but with a deeper love than they had before, a love more calm, more pure, more peaceful, more unselfish, more divine. Beloved, are you letting Him so refine you, so transform you, so anticipate in you His own coming and millennial life and glory?

Or again, perhaps He is teaching you the higher grace of love, and leading you through the thirteenth chapter of first Corinthians. Some of you know how slowly you get through it. Perhaps you have got the long-suffering and kindness, the humility and modesty of the fourth verse. Perhaps you have got through the unselfishness of the fifth verse, but have you got to the "not provoked," to the "thinketh no evil?" Perhaps you can bear all things in the seventh verse with a "grin-and-bear-it" stoicism, but have you got into the next clause, "believeth all things, hopeth all things?" Have you got into the spirit that so refuses to believe evil that there is really nothing to bear, that cuts the sinews

of your troubles by ignoring them and refusing to believe them really, and by looking at the people that have wronged you
with such a loving trustfulness that you
will not believe evil of them if it seem to
be true, and if you cannot quite believe that
it is not so, you will, like your heavenly
Father, say, "It should not be, and I will
think of them as if it were not true?"

For my own sake I always try to refuse
to believe it if I can, and if I cannot believe
good of people at the present, it is an infinite comfort to me to ask the Lord to make
it true, and then believe that He will make
it true, and then to hope for them with that
confidence which enables me to count the
things which are not as if they were, and
henceforth think of the erring one in the light
of my hope, in the light of their own future,
as though already in heaven and the perfection and glory of the Father's life.

Beloved, that erring brother some day
will be brighter than the sun, and you will
love him without a recollection of your

present grievances against him. Think of
this now as if it were so, and so anticipate
the future, and so rise out of the present
that you shall act under the influence of
that which shall be, and you can so labor
and pray to make it real.

And so about the eight verse, "charity
never faileth." You have a great deal of
love, and you uniformly triumph, but once
in a while you sort of claim the privilege of
a temporary failure. You do not think it
very wrong if you occasionally break down,
and so your weak link destroys the entire
chain. God is leading you through this to
that victory which never fails, so that love
which goes forth exclaiming, "Thanks be
unto God which always causeth us to
triumph through Christ Jesus," and making
manifest the Saviour. of His knowledge by
us in every place.

Or again, the Refiner may be taking you
through the experience of patience, and
strengthening you with all might according
to His glorious power unto all patience and

long-suffering with joyfulness. Perhaps you
have got the patience and the long-suffering,
but have you got the joyfulness? And so we
might take all the lessons, and trace His
gentle leading and teaching through the discipline of our spiritual life as He is bringing
us closer and closer to His own glorious
likeness.

Beloved, are we letting Him? A jeweler
once told a lady that he kept the silver in
the fire until he could see his face in it; and
so the great Refiner sits down quietly,
slowly, at the crucible where our hearts are
consuming, and waits till He can see His
image in our hearts, in our souls, and then
He dismisses the firemen, carries away the
ashes, stops the flame, and takes the silver
and pours it into the mould of something
lovely and heavenly, where it becomes a
vessel for His grace and love, or perhaps as
flagons to carry His wine and water to His
perishing, suffering children, for "He is refining and purifying us as silver is tried,
that the sons of Levi may offer unto Him

an offering in righteousness;" and the service of sanctified men and women is immeasurably more precious to God in its most trivial forms than all we can do or give when our hearts are swept by earthly passion, or influenced by selfish or unholy motives.

CHAPTER XIV.

THE BAPTIZER.

"Upon whom thou shalt see the Spirit descending, and remaining upon Him, the same is He which baptizeth with the Holy Ghost." John i: 33.

THIS is one of the names given to our dear Lord, and it is especially appropriate for this sacred day, which, in the calender of a portion of the church of Christ, is devoted to the special recognition of the third person of the Godhead, the blessed Holy Spirit. It is becoming that we should greatly honor the Holy Ghost; for He never honors Himself, but ever holds up the person of Jesus Christ, and hides behind the glory of Him whom He loves to reveal. It is not, however, of the Holy Ghost directly that this passage speaks, but of Him who sends the Holy Ghost, "He that baptizeth with the Holy Ghost," our blessed Lord, to whom we owe this most-precious gift of the New Testament dispensation.

I. IN WHAT SENSE CHRIST BABTIZETH WITH THE HOLY GHOST.

The Spirit is His gift as He is the Father's gift. The greatest gift of the Old Testament was Jesus; the greatest gift of Jesus was the Spirit. The Father sends the Son; the Son baptizeth with the Spirit; and the Spirit brings both the Father and the Son into our heart and life.

1. Jesus is the giver of the Holy Ghost inasmuch as He has removed the hindrances to the coming of the Spirit into our hearts. The great hindrance was sin. The Holy Ghost is just the presence of God, and God cannot dwell in an unholy temple any more than Noah's dove could rest upon the earth while the floods of judgment and the carcasses of corrupt flesh covered the earth. Not until the flood was passed and all flesh had died, and the earth was cleansed by its great baptism of judgment, could the dove

rest, not merely for a moment upon the bows of the olive trees, but all over the land, to fly abroad, and build its nest, and rear its broods wherever it could find a sheltering branch. So the Holy Ghost, under the Old Testament, could not rest in the heart of men. Often He visited them, even as the dove went forth from the ark; often He revealed the olive branch of peace and covenant; often He came to the hearts of men with divine light, and life, and help; but the human breast was not His home until after Jesus had finished His work of atonement. But when, through the cross of Calvary, the judgment of sin was accomplished, and, in the death of the substitute, sinful man was recognized as dead to the flesh, as judged, crucified; then He went forth to rest and reside on earth, and to make the hearts of men His home.

Just as soon as through the ascension of Jesus it was demonstrated that sin was judged and God was satisfied for guilty man, immediately the Holy Ghost came down from heaven. 'And so in the individual life, just as soon as sin is confessed and judged, and the blood of the great sacrifice is appropriated, and Jesus Christ accepted as the propitiation and the cleansing of the heart, into the holy temple of our inmost being the blessed Comforter loves to come, and to dwell as our guest, our friend, our guide, our Master, the representative to us of God, and the executive in us and for us, of His holy will. To Jesus we owe all this. But for His redeeming work, the blessed presence of God could never come to dwell within us; but now the message has gone forth to every sinful soul, "Repent and be baptized in the name of the Lord Jesus, for the remission of sins, and ye shall receive the gift of the Holy Ghost."

Beloved, have you accepted the great atonement, have you received the cleansing blood, have you been reconciled and sanctified, and has the way been opened by the precious blood of the great High Priest into the Holy of Holies of your inmost being, for

the Shekinah of His glory to shine within,
and reveal the light of the knowledge of the
glory of God in the face of Jesus? Is there
any cloud of sin hiding and hindering that
divine indwelling? Oh, He is able to clear
it all away. Come to His blessed feet, come
to His sprinkled blood, come to His throne
of grace, come to the great sacrifice, come
to the cross of Calvary, come to the great
High Priest, come to Jesus, and He will
cleanse you by His blood, and baptize you
with His Holy Spirit.

2. Jesus baptizeth with the Holy Ghost
inasmuch as He received the Holy Ghost
into His own person, and for three years
and a half walked through Galilean Judea
"in the Spirit," which He now gives to us;
receiving the third person of the Godhead
into personal union with Himself, so that
He could send Him forth, not as another
Spirit, but as His own Spirit. This is very
precious and truly wonderful. The Holy
Ghost is not to us now what He would have
been before Jesus came, and what He was

under the Old Testáment, purely the
Spirit of Deity; but He is, if we can understand what it means, the Spirit that dwelt
in the human and divine Christ; the Spirit
that (if we may say it with reverence) was
softened and in some sense humanized by
union with Jesus; the Spirit that loved John
and Mary, that took the little children to
His bosom, that compassionated the multitude, that wept for Jerusalem, that said to
the poor woman, "Go and sin no mo:e;"
that whispered, "Let not your heart be
troubled;" that talked with the woman of
Samaria, that forgave and restored Peter,
that overlooked all Thomas' unbelief, that
bore so patiently the shame of the judgment
hall, and endured the agony of the cross,
that walked and talked on the way to
Emmaus, so simply, and yet with such
human tenderness and nearness. Oh, how
near it brings Him to receive Him as the
Spirit of our precious Christ! And so Jesus
received Him and spake all His words, and
did all His works through the Spirit; and

now He gives to us the very same Spirit
that dwelt in Him.   And so in Romans the
apostle speaks of the Spirit of Christ, and
says, "If Christ be in you the body is dead
because of sin, but the Spirit is life because
of righteousness," and "If any man have
not the Spirit of Christ, he is none of His."

Beloved, He is waiting to-day to give you
His own very Spirit, to breathe upon you
and say, "Receive ye the Holy Ghost."
And you may take Him warm from the
bosom of Jesus, sweet as the breath of His
love, pure as the light of His holiness, mighty
as the strength of His omnipotence, and, in
some sense, colored and softened by the
very humanity of our incarnate Lord.

3. Jesus baptizes with the Holy Ghost in
the sense that He distinctly sent Him on the
day of Pentecost, from heaven to earth.   It
was His promise that He would do so.   "If
I go not away the Comforter will not come;
but if I depart, I will send Him unto you."
And so Peter, speaking of His coming, says,
"He, having received of the Father the

promise of the Holy Ghost, hath now shed forth this, which ye now see and hear." This was a distinct and actual transaction which involved the most stupendous issues and relations. On that day and in that moment a real person, a divine person, actually changed His residence and removed from heaven to earth, and has ever since resided, not in heaven, but in this world. With the sound of that mighty rushing wind, a procession as glorious as the ascension of Jesus took place. The Holy Dove, the mighty Paraclete, came down from heaven to return no more till the dispensation of the gospel shall have closed; and from that hour his residence has been in this world in the hearts of Christ's people, and the sacred sanctuary of His body, the church.

Let us fully realize this. The Spirit is not now in heaven, and we need never ask Him to come from heaven; but He is present, and we have only to receive Him, for He has already come. The mighty baptism has been commanded and imparted; and, just as the air is charged with electricity and you have but to absorb it from the atmosphere, just as the atmosphere is saturated with moisture, and the cool pitcher has only to absorb the dew; so the Holy Ghost is all around us, the spaces about us are filled with His presence, His ear is within whispering distance of every heart, and we have but to become receiving vessels adjusted to His touch, and He flows in to fill every channel of our being as naturally as the air enters the open lungs, as the light floods the lifted window, as the sun shines wherever there is any object to receive his radiance. Beloved, the Holy Ghost has come, the day of Pente-cost is past, the Spirit of God is here, will you receive Him?

4. But there is yet a personal baptism with the Holy Ghost which must come to each heart for itself. To each of us must be applied personally the great atonement, to each of us must come the actual presence of the comforter, and Jesus is the one that will bring this to pass. It is not the Holy

Ghost you are to pray to, but it is the Saviour. It is He that baptizeth with the Holy Ghost. Go to Jesus for Him, put yourself at His dear feet, take Him as your Saviour, take Him as your Sanctifier, trust Him to give you this most precious gift, claim it, and refuse to let Him go without its fullness, hold fast to His loving feet, claim your birthright, your redemption right, what He so longs to give you, obey His voice; follow His directions, thank Him for the faintest touch that answers your prayer, follow on in the light that He gives, even in a gleam of radiance, and you shall know the Lord in all the fullness of His glory and love, and eternally praise Him who baptizeth with the Holy Ghost.

II. WHAT IS INVOLVED IN THIS GREAT BAPTISM AND BLESSING.

1. It is different from the conversion of the soul and the work of the Holy Spirit in regeneration. That is the birth of the soul, this is the baptism. Just as Jesus Himself

was born of the Spirit in Mary's bosom, but thirty years later was baptized of the Spirit on the banks of the Jordan, so each of us is born of the Spirit in the moment of our conversion, but we are baptized of the Spirit when we yield ourselves fully to Christ, and, like Him on Jordan's banks, enter upon our life-work for God.

2. It is a direct personal coming of God's Spirit into the heart, and a complete possessing of it by the Spirit for God and His holy will and work.   The first, the conversion of the soul, which He may do at a distance, or by a momentary act. The baptism of the Spirit is God's residence in the soul, which is a closer union, and a more continuous communion and working. The one is the building of a house, and I may build a hundred houses, the other is my residence in the house, and the making of that house my abode.

3. What are the effects of this divine incoming and occupancy? Let us trace them briefly as Christ Himself reveals them in His own promise.

d. "At that day (*i.e.*, the day when the Comforter comes) ye shall know that I am in the Father, and ye in me, and I in you." That is to say, the coming of the Holy Spirit will give reality, vividness and intense consciousness to our union with Jesus Christ. We will not be so conscious that we have received the Spirit as that Jesus is dwelling in our hearts and bringing the Father with Him. We shall not believe or hope, but we shall intensely know by the deepest spiritual cognition and consciousness, by an intuition deeper than any emotional impression or feeling, that "He is in us, and we in Him," and our life is part of His, and His life is part of ours forever.

Do we not long for this? Does not Jesus sometimes seem far away? Is it not difficult for you to conceive and grasp His personal reality? Does your heart not hunger for a keen, sweet, constant sense of His substantial reality? Oh! will you not cry for the Holy Ghost to make you know that "He is in the Father, and you in Him, and He in you." It is His own promise. Hold Him to it, and claim it of Him this day in all His fullness. This is the deepest need of your spiritual life, to know Jesus as abiding in you, to understand the secret, which is "Christ in you the hope of glory;" to have no doubt of it, no vague reaching out for it, but a deep abiding rest in His abiding love. Beloved, claim your privilege. Blessed Holy Ghost, make Jesus real to us, and let us know that we are in Him, and that He is in us, as never before, in the deep eternal rest, faith, fellowship and love.

b. The baptism of the Spirit will bring you instruction and light; for "He shall teach you all things." Our minds need to be instructed, as well as our spirits united to Christ. Our thought needs to be directed in the fullness of divine truth. Our understanding needs to be illuminated in the knowledge of God and His Word. Our Bible needs to be made plain and living to us; and all this the Spirit does. How in a moment He lights up a passage with a

strange vividness, which we had often
read, and which we had intellectually un-
derstood, but had never felt the power of!
How plain He makes the subject of sanctification by a single touch of heavenly light!
How easy it seems to us to claim Him as a
Healer when the truth is brought home to
the heart by the Holy Ghost, not as a
theory, but as a living light from heaven for
our suffering life!

Not only does He teach, but He continues
to teach; and He repeats His teaching; for
He will "bring all things to your remembrance, whatsoever I have said unto
you." In a moment of perplexity He will
suggest to us with strange appropriateness
the very thought and word that will bring
us direction. In the hour of temptation He
will bring to our remembrance the promise
that will deliver and overcome the adversary,
"the sword of the Spirit, which is the Word
of God." In the dark night of sorrow He
will shed the bright light of His comfort,
and the star of promise will shine with a

brightness we could not see by day. In the
time of service He will bring to our remembrance the truth that we need to speak.
"He will waken our ear morning by morning to hear as the learned, that we may
know how to speak a word in season to him
that is weary," and "it shall be given you
in that same hour what ye shall say, and
what ye shall speak."

As we kneel by the side of the inquirer
and the penitent He will give to us the appropriate message. As we meet the as-
sults and the keen criticisms of man, He
will enable us to know what we ought to
answer every one, and will let our speech
be always with grace, seasoned with salt.
And we will often wonder at the strange
simplicity and sweetness with which in-
tuitively our thoughts come to us, and
some one seems to be thinking in us without
our trying. Oh, the blessed help of the
Holy Ghost's suggestive ministry ! Beloved,
do you want this inward monitor, this continual guide, this sweet voice, this whisper-

ing presence, this tender mother, and guide and friend? Oh! come to Jesus, who baptizeth with the Holy Ghost, and receive His richest gift this day.

c. He will not only teach, but "He will guide us into all truth." This is more than teaching; this is the direction of our steps, the leading of our feet into the paths of His holy will. Wisdom is more than knowledge, and guidance more than instruction. Wisdom is that which shows us where we are and ought to go, and keeps us from error and mistake; and this is the blessed Spirit's special ministry—to guide the trusting and obedient heart and let it make no mistake, "For He is able to keep us from stumbling, and to present us faultless before the presence of His glory with exceeding joy." He will show us the way in which we ought to go. "He will lead us in a straight way, wherein we shall not stumble." Oh, how often we have erred, and how sad the consequences of our mistakes! How our feet have been wounded by the thorns, and our hearts have been pierced by the stings that have followed our disobedience, when we knew not why we stumbled! But the blessed Spirit will give us light and keep us right, if we will but trust Him and follow Him, and receive Him in His fullness.

d. He will give us succes in all our work for Him, "For after that He is come, He will convict the world of sin, of righteousness, and of judgment." We cannot convict men of sin. We may pierce them with a thousand accusings, we may sting them with our reproaches, we may warn them with our most solemn messages, we may plead with them with the utmost pathos and tenderness, but we cannot bring conviction to their consciences. But He can. He can make a single word enter the heart like a barbed arrow, and slay the pride and self-confidence, and lay the sinner in the dust. He can make a single look send Peter down to weep the tender tears that melted, but did not break his heart.

And He can convict them of righteousness. He can show them the Saviour as their Righteousness, and He can enable the poor sinner, as we point him to Jesus, to "behold the Lamb of God, which taketh away the sin of the world," and to trust himself in His loving arms, and to take him as His own Saviour, and to know that He does save, forgive, and sweetly accept forever. He can show the poor, struggling heart God's righteousness; Jesus as the Sanctifier, the Keeper, the Rest, and enable us to commit our souls to His keeping, and know that what we have committed to Him He is able to keep against that day, and so go forward in victory and praise.

And He can convict the world of judgment, "because the prince of this world is judged." That is, it seems to us, He can make the poor, baffled, beaten heart to know that Satan is overcome, that through Jesus he is a conquered foe, and that now we need fear him no more, but may stand in complete victory, and know that neither life, nor death, nor earth, nor hell can ever separate us from the love of Christ.

e. Again, He gives us power. "For ye shall receive power after the Holy Ghost is come upon you," was the Master's parting word, "and ye shall be witnesses unto me." This is not the power of human persuasion or natural ability of any kind, but it is the divine power working through us. It is that which makes our words and acts effectual. It is that strange influence which makes things tell, and often brings out the very little things mighty and lasting results. This made Peter's sermon on the day of Pentecost, although the utterance of a few simple words of truth, the means of converting thousands of souls. This made Paul's ministry mighty through God to the establishment of Christianity in all the world. And this will make the weak things to confound the things that are mighty; the things that are despised, the foolish things, yea, the things that are not, to bring to naught the things that are, that the weakness of God may be stronger than men and the foolishness of God wiser than men; for Christ is the power of God and the wisdom of God through the Holy Ghost.

f. Again, the Holy Ghost gives us courage. "Perceiving the boldness of Peter and John, they took knowledge of them that they had been with Jesus," and so "God hath not given us the spirit of fear." The Holy Ghost is courage. He makes the heart strong, and sets the face like a flint in the steps of faith, and the path of duty, and the battle of the Lord. Timid one, would you be brave; fearful one, would you be strong; shrinking one, would you stand firm? "Receive ye the Holy Ghost."

g. Again, He gives us wisdom. This was the endowment of Stephen and his brethren. This was the apostle's assurance to Timothy, "God hath given us the Spirit of a sound mind." It was He who guided and governed the apostolic church. It was He who enabled Paul to form his plans and purposes. Especially do we read in the life

of Paul that at a certain crisis he purposed
in the Spirit that he would adopt a certain
plan of work, and pursue certain lines in
his missionary journey; and, although
every influence on earth and every power
from beneath, seemed leagued together to
defeat his purpose, and even the very
saints of God and the prophets of inspira-
tion tried to turn him aside, that purpose
which had been formed "in the Spirit"
was literally fulfilled, and he was held to it
with the tenacity of victorious faith. So
He will guide our plans, establish our purposes, and accomplish our highest, holiest
desires for the glory and work of God.

h. Again, He is the Spirit of love. After
the gifts of power referred to, in the twelfth
chapter of first Corinthians, the apostle
tells us that the greatest of these is love;
and it is emphatic, it is very important to
notice that the terms in which this is spoken
of, distinctly imply that it is not a human
virtue or the exercise of any will of our
own, or any feeling of our natural heart,

but it is a distinct and supernatural gift of the Spirit.

The word for love is *charitas*, and the word for the gift of grace is, *charis*, so that it is distinctly recognized as a divine gift, and not in any sense a personal quality. He will give us this wondrous love in all its fullness, sweetness and victorious power.

Would you have the love that suffers long and is kind? Receive the Holy Ghost. Would you have the love that vaunteth not itself and is not puffed up, but acts ever with sweet and lowly meekness? Receive the Holy Ghost. Would you have the love that doth not behave itself unseemly, and cannot do a rude act or speak a hard and harmful word? Receive the Holy Ghost. Would you have the love that seeketh not her own, but is ever self-forgetful, lives for others and for God without thinking for itself? Receive the baptism of the Holy Ghost. Would you have the love that thinketh no evil, that allows no thought of suspicion ever to touch you, that imagines no wrong in a brother, that would rather be deceived than think evil, that believeth all things with simple, artless confidence, that hopeth all things, even though the present seems all wrong, and covers the future with faith, and prayer, and blessing, even for the unworthy heart? Would you know the rest of being saved from thinking of your brother's faults, and living in a constant atmosphere of sweetest confidence and innocency, and harmless like a little nestling dove? Receive from Jesus His greatest gift. Receive from the Spirit His richest, His highest grace, the grace of heavenly love. Would you have the love that never faileth, that never again is going to let you stumble, never again pierce your heart with a thorn, never again to sting you with that with which you stung your brother? Come to Him who baptizeth with the Holy Ghost, and let Him put into you to-day the same Spirit that made Him holy, harmless, undefiled and separate from sinners, the Christ of love.

i. Again, He is the Spirit that shields you

from temptation, and gives you victory in the hour of conflict; for "when the enemy cometh in like a flood, the Spirit of the Lord shall lift up a standard against him," and He will so fill you with His own presence that the shafts shall not stick, but He in you shall resist, repel, and hurl back all the wild billows of the adversary's rage. Like the red-hot iron which repels the slightest particle of water or dust from adhering to it because of its heat, so the kindled Spirit shall throw off the touches of the enemy, and you shall move on in glory and victory, and "He shall be a wall of fire around you, and the glory in the midst."

j. Again, He is the Spirit of prayer, for "the Spirit maketh intercession within us· with groanings which cannot be uttered." This is our highest service for God; and they who are ever filled with the Spirit, will be able to touch the throne with the very power of God, and the prayer that rises from your heart will be a divine power, and He will know instinctively that it has the answer even before it asks, because it is the thought and will of God reflected back again to Him from whom it came. Oh! would you have the power that will move heaven and earth, that will prevail with God and man, that will take the fullness of Christ's promises for these last days, that will meet the mighty conflicts that are coming in victorious omnipotence, beloved, come to Him who baptizeth with the Holy Ghost, and be endued with power from on high.

We are in the days of supernatural conflict, we are touching the borders of the tribulation times. We are feeling the dragon-wing that is in a little while to overshadow the earth and blot out the very light of the sun. We are nearing these dark hours from which Christ is to call up His own elect. Deeper, stronger, subtler than ever before; more penetrating, more mighty are the weapons that are against us, and the forms that assail us and resist us. We must be endued with power from on high. We must be encased in the armor of fire.

We must be filled with the living God. We must be baptized with the Holy Ghost, and baptized as we never have been before with the all-encompassing presence of God, where no joint in the harness can let in an arrow of the enemy, and no slip for a single second give Him the slightest advantage. Oh! thou who baptizeth with the Holy Ghost, hear thy people's prayer, robe them in thine own omnipotence, clothe them in the garments of thy fire, baptize them with the fullness of the seven-fold Holy Ghost, and keep them abiding in thee, and walking in the Spirit every breath and every step.

k. Again, He is the Spirit of hope. "Now the God of patience fill you with all joy and peace in believing, that ye may abound in hope through the power of the Holy Ghost." He, and He alone, can take the fears from out of your heart, and the shadows from off your future. He can thrust away the dark clouds of dread that blot out all light and confidence, and that cover everything with the dismal shadow of despair. He can illumine your own path through life with sweet and heavenly confidence. He can unfold to you the vision of the land that is very far off. He can show the stretches of the outreaching of God's blessed promises for you, and all His glorious work for you. Yes, He can show you the coming of the King in His glory, and even touch your heart with the thrill of personal hope, and the expectation of beholding Him with these mortal eyes, and preparing this world for His glorious advent.

III. WHAT IS IMPLIED IN RECEIVING THIS BAPTISM.

1. The very thought of baptism suggests the deeply solemn thought of death and resurrection. Baptism is burial and a new life; and, therefore, to receive the fullness of the Holy Spirit there must be death; the death of much, nay, the death of all that will and can die, for only that which is imperishable ought to live. The gold cannot be burned, therefore you need not fear to

die in the arms of Jesus to everything that is capable of dying; and everything that will not die is safe, for only that which is divine can stand the fire of God. Yield yourself unto His death in all the fullness of His thought, and then rise into life in all the fullness of His will, and be baptized into the Spirit. Therefore you, that have died to self and earth, have received, and will receive in that measure the fullness of His Spirit and life, even in those very places where you have most truly died. And you, that have not received the fullness of His baptism, are, perhaps, hindered because in some place you have not died with your Lord, or having died, have not risen again into His resurrection life; for there comes a call to arise as well as to die, and the voice of heaven, which says, "Arise, shine, for thy light is come, and the glory of the Lord is risen upon thee."

2. The term baptism suggests great fullness. It is into an ocean that you are baptized. It is not a sprinkled drop, but it

is a great unfathomable sea, and God is calling us to go out into the deeps of Himself. Too long we stayed in the shallow surf, swept by its surges, defiled by its miry waters, and beaten by its mighty breakers. Out beyond are the depths of calm, the fullness unfathomable. Let us launch out into the deep, out into the fullness of God.

3. Again, this figure suggests great simplicity of receiving the Holy Ghost. It is easy to be baptized. You have just to let yourself go and sink into the floods, or lie restfully in the hand that upholds you, or on the bosom of the wave whereon you repose. So it is a very simple thing to receive the Holy Ghost. It is trust. How little we trust the Spirit! How we strive, and strain, and do violence to nature in the struggle after some deep filling, when in quietness and restfulness we might receive His heavenly life and influence.

The rock of Kadesh was the type of the Holy Spirit's deeper overflowing; and the command of Moses was to speak to the rock, but on no account to strike it; and his striking the rock became a sin and offence, which did not hinder the water coming, but hindered his full blessing. There is something very suggestive in this simple thought of speaking to the rock. It is the attitude of simple trust, and confidence, and quietness. Let us speak to the rock. Let us draw near in the desert, amid the hot and burning sands, thirsty, weary, fainting, everything around us wretched and sad. The face of yonder rock seems hard as flint, but in its bosom are stores of infinite refreshing. It needs no violent grasp, or voice, or touch to bring them forth. Speak the word of simple trust. Speak to the rock, and lo! the waters will gush forth in streams of refreshing, and you shall drink, and you shall lave in their cool tides until the wilderness and the solitary place shall be glad, and the desert shall blossom as the rose. It is Jesus who is that rock He is standing before thee now. He that baptiz-

eth thee with the Holy Ghost, He loves
thee, He redeemed thee, He will never fail
if thou wilt trust Him.   Trust Him for the
Holy Ghost, and sweetly receive His infinite
fullness, that thou mayest have, to give to a
thirsty world, the fullness which He has
given thee.

Fainting in the desert, Israel's thousands stand
At the rock of Kadesh, hark ! the Lord's command,
Speak to the rock, bid the waters flow,
Strike not its bosom, opened long ago,
Speak to the rock 'till the waters flow.

Blessed Rock of Ages, thou art open still,
Blessed Holy Spirit all our being fill;
Still thou dost say, wherefore struggle so ?
Call to the Spirit, whisper soft and low,
Speak to the rock, bid the waters flow.

Oh, for trust most simple, fully to believe,
Oh, for hearts more childlike, freely to receive;
E'en as a babe, on its mother's breast,
So, on thy bosom let my spirit rest,
Filled with thy life, with thy blessing blest.

Speak to the rock, bid the waters flow,
Doubt not the Spirit, given long ago;
Take what He waiteth, freely to bestow,
Drink 'till its fullness all thy being know.

CHAPTER XV.

CHRIST THE LIVING VINE.

"I am the vine, ye are the branches: He that abideth in me, and I in him, the same bringeth forth much fruit: for without me ye can do nothing." John xiv: 5.

THE vine is the most important production of the vegetable creation; therefore it has been used by the devil for greater harm than anything that God ever made, for Satan ever loves to steal God's best gifts. God has always used the vine as the symbol of the most sacred things, its juice being the type of Christ's blood, and its stems and branches the most perfect figure of the mystery of Godliness, Christ's union with His people. The Scriptures give us no profounder view of Christian life than these verses contain. Let us look first at the spiritual teaching, and then at some illustrations of this in the figure itself.

I. UNION WITH JESUS.

The first truth conveyed in the Master's teaching is that of union with Jesus. There are two sides to this. The first is "in me," the second, "I in you." The first expresses our justification; the second our deeper union with Christ in sanctification. To be in Christ is to accept Him as our Saviour, and to be justified through His blood and righteousness, accepted by the Father for His sake, and received into all His rights and privileges, as the children of God and the redeemed family of Christ. There are two races, the Adam race, and the Christ race. We are all born in Adam, and in Adam all die, but all who are in Christ shall be made alive. And so we came into Christ by receiving Him as our Head and our Saviour, and being born again into His life through His Holy Spirit. Every believer is in Christ, and there is no condemnation to them that are in Christ Jesus, for we are made accepted in the Beloved.

To be in Christ has reference rather to our

standing than our actual experience. It de-
notes the relationship between us and Christ,
rather than the actual life, and realization
of His presence and communion. Of course,
it will bring an actul experience ; but that is
more fully described by the other phrase, "I
in you." This is the other side of our union
with Jesus. It is that which brings Him
personally into actual touch with us, for
this is the great mystery of redemption, that
Christ actually comes to dwell in the heart
that is in Him, making it His personal residence and chosen home, and filling it with
His love and joy and purity. In the previous chapter He had already explained this
union, and declared that it would be the first
result of the Holy Spirit's coming into the
heart, that He should reveal it, consummate
it, and make it intensely real to our consciousness. "At that day," He says (the day
of the Holy Spirit's coming to abide with us),
"ye shall know that I am in my Father, and
ye in me, and I in you." And still later He
added, "If a man love me, He will keep my

commandments, and I will love Him and
manifest myself unto Him." And then He
adds still further, "My Father will love him,
and we will come in unto him, and make
our abode with him." This is the glorious
reality to which He refers in this figure. "I
in you."

Again and again it is unfolded in the later
teachings of the New Testament. The apostle
declares that it was His great mission to unfold it, "the mystery hid from ages and
generations, which is Christ in you, the
hope of glory. It is the last appeal of the
ascended Lord to the churches in Asia, that
they will open the door and let Him come in,
"and sup with them, and they with Him."
It is the last thought in His own intercessory
prayer as He commits His dear disciples to
His Father's keeping," and prays that "the
love wherewith thou hast loved me may be
in them, and I in them." It is the secret of
peace; for He says, "My peace I give unto
you." It is the secret of joy; for He says,
"My joy shall remain in you." It is the

secret of faith ; for the apostle says, "Christ liveth in me, and the life I now live in the flesh I live by the faith of the Son of God, who loved me, and gave Himself for me." It is the secret of holiness ; for "Christ is made unto us of God sanctification." It is the secret of power; for "I can do all things through Christ which strengtheneth me." It is the secret of all things, the solution of all problems, the spring of all spiritual blessings, for they are all in Christ Jesus. Such then, are the two sides of our union with Christ, "He in us," and "we in Him," even as the branch is in the vine, the members are in the body, the Son is in the Father.

2. The next truth conveyed here is communion. "Abide in me." One with Him we must act according to the fact of our union, and keep up the fellowship and mutual relationships involved in this union. When the wife is married it is expected that she will act accordingly, and maintain the attitude of a wife by fellowship and dependence. When a partnership is formed between

two human beings, they are expected to co-operate according to the agreement; and when the soul and Christ become united, there are certain actual relationships, and mutual fellowships, which are to be constantly maintained. This is spoken of as abiding, and upon the steadiness and simplicity of this depends the happiness and power of our Christian life. One of the attitudes implied in abiding, is dependence. It is the habit of continually looking to Christ for everything; for He says, "apart from me ye can do nothing." We are to continually distrust ourselves, and feel our utter inability to think a right thought, and to look to Him in utter helplessness, and yet in trustful reliance for every breath and thought and feeling, taking our life each moment from Him, both for soul and body, bringing every temptation to Him, every need, every desire, and living really by Him and on Him, as a babe upon its mother.

Another idea expressed by abiding is fellowship in prayer. There is a near atmosphere of prayer and communion which may be ceaselessly maintained between the soul and the Saviour. Its spirit is very subtle, its home is like the Holy of Holies, its atmosphere is pure and fragrant as the inner chamber of the sanctuary. It is sullied by a breath of sin, it is broken by a thought of distrust and disobedience. It is a very close place in the "secret of the most High, and under the shadow of the Almighty." There it is that we learn to pray without ceasing, and in everything give thanks, and like Enoch, walk with God.

Another thought suggested by abiding is the momentary life. It is not a life of drift and impulse, not a life in which we act on general principles, but a moment by moment dependence upon Christ. It is simply finding that the life that can be maintained for one moment can be equally maintained for innumerable moments. It is just living out the simple word of Paul in Colossians, "As ye have received Christ Jesus the Lord, so walk ye in Him."

There are certain principles affecting this life of abiding. It is a principle of human nature, that a succession of momentary acts repealed for a certain time, produces a habit of thought and feeling, and that which at first is a somewhat labored purpose and requires much vigilance to maintain, gradually grows into a delightful habit of dependence, and the momentary acts of abiding are so simple that they are like the breathing of the lungs.

Our abiding depends upon our obedience. "If ye keep my commandments ye shall abide in my love." We shall find ourselves, sometimes, in positions where we cannot touch Christ for help and blessing, and the reason is that there is some obstacle between us and our Lord, and some disobedience or sin which must be removed. It is a matter not only of trust, but also of rightness, and we will find that our peace and communion depend upon walking closely with Him and hearkening unto His holy will. It is if His words abide in us that we have the promise,

"Ye shall ask what ye will." He will show us faithfully the disobedience or the cloud, and will enable us to put it aside, and then will restore to us the joy of His communion and the fullness of His very Spirit. So let us abide in Him.

II. THE EFFECTS OF ABIDING.

1. Cleansing. "Now ye are clean through the word that I have spoken unto you." This word was spoken in the thirteenth chapter. It came through the washing of the disciples' feet. And so still He waits to wash our feet from the stains of the way, and except He wash we have no part with Him. We must be cleansed, and keep clean in order to maintain our communion.

2. The second effect of abiding is fruitfulness. "He that abideth in me, and I in Him, the same bringeth forth much fruit." Fruit is different from effort. The farmer toils in his garden as he prunes and waters the tree and cultivates the ground, but the tree has no toil or effort, but with sponta-

neons freedom sends forth its leaves, its blossoms, and its fruits. And so in the Christian life there is no effort in bearing fruit if we have the life of Christ within us. It springs spontaneously from the full heart. The mother of liberty and love, and the fruit of the spirit is love, joy, peace, long-suffering, and all the sweet grapes of Christian life, besides the reproducing of ourselves in the lives and souls we bring to Christ.

3. The next effect of abiding is answered prayer. "We shall ask what we will, and it shall be done unto us, if we abide in Him, and His words abide in us." The reason of this is, our prayer will be His prayer, our desire will be His desire, our thought will be His thought, our faith will be His faith, and we will know as we ask that He accepts and gives because He prompts the prayer as He walks with us.

4. The next effect of His abiding is His love. "Continue ye, or abide ye, in my love. As the Father hath loved me, even so have I loved you." It is a blessed thing to

live in love.   Some people live in an atmosphere of constant duty.   Our privilege is to
live in an atmosphere of love, and to be so
pervaded with the dear love of Jesus that we
shall know that He is always pleased with
us, though we often make mistakes, yet He
accepts our true heart and loves us with all
His heart.

5. Again, abiding will bring us joy.
" These these things have I spoken unto you,
that my joy might remain with you, and
that your joy might be full."   If He is in us,
His joy will be in us, and our hearts will
spring and sing with a gladness not our own,
but wholly prompted by His Spirit within
us.

6. Again, abiding will lead to obedience,
implicit and constant obedience ; for He says,
"ye are my friends if ye do whatsoever I
command you."   This is not obedience usually, but it is obedience unconditionally and
under all circumstances to "whatsoever I
command you."

7. Again, abiding will bring us His per-

sonal and confidential friendship. "Ye are my friends, if ye do whatsoever I command you. Henceforth I call you not servants; for the servant knoweth not what His Lord doeth, but I have called you friends, for all things that I have heard of my Father I have made known unto you." It is delightful to walk with Jesus in holy confidence, and know that we have His freest communion, and that He treats us as His beloved ones.

8. Again, abiding will lead to permanence in our work. "Ye have not chosen me, but I have chosen you, and ordained you that ye should go and bring forth fruit, and that your fruit should remain." That which springs from Him shall last, and shall meet us again, not only here, but in the life to come. These are the blessings of abiding. How precious, how-complete, how eternal! Oh, that we may not miss one of them, but live so closely to our Lord that we shall have all the good pleasure of His goodness, and the fullness of His blessing!

III. SOME ILLUSTRATIONS OF THESE TRUTHS
FROM THE FIGURE OF THE VINE
AND ITS BRANCHES.

1. The vine and the branch are one. The vine it not separate from the branch, but the vine includes the branch. And so Christ is not the vine separated from us; but the full Christ consists of Christ the Head, and us the body. Christ has become forever so identified with us that He needs us to complete Himself. His joy is not complete without us. His glory is fulfilled in our glory and blessing.

2. The branches need much pruning. Much of the gardener's work is to prune down the growth that is excessive, and that would simply produce show and not fruit. And so our gentle and gracious Father cuts back much of our life that would simply grow into selfish luxuriance, and only leaves that which can bear real fruit unto Him. Let us trust Him. He is not destroying the tree, but only correcting it and its form, and enriching its fruitfulness, its value.

3. The branches that bear fruit in the vine are the fresh ones. The little shoots that shall spring forth this spring, they, and they only bear the fruit. The old dried branches bear no fruit. They support the ones that do. And so there must be constant freshness and growth to our spiritual life, if there is to be fruit. Only that which God is really doing in you, and doing to-day, will bear fruit to others. You cannot take the experience of a year ago, and serve the Lord with that, but you must know Christ to-day in fresh and ceaseless communion, or you cannot accomplish any effective work for Him.

4. The vine is of no use for anything else but for fruit. It cannot be made into lumber or furniture; it has but one purpose. And so the Christian, especially the consecrated Christian, is worthless and useless, unless to abide in Christ and bear fruit for God. Oh, that we may continually abide and bear much fruit, for "herein is the Father glorified, that ye bear much fruit,"

and the Son satisfied for the travail of His soul and the sacrifice of His life.

ND - #0042 - 240223 - C0 - 229/152/15 [17] - CB - 9780483577633 - Gloss Lamination